Education, Dialogue and Hermeneutics

Also available from Continuum

Philosophy of Education, Richard Pring
Theory and Practice of Education, David A. Turner
Education After Dewey, Paul Fairfield

Education, Dialogue and Hermeneutics

Edited by
Paul Fairfield

Continuum International Publishing Group
A Bloomsbury company
50 Bedford Square
London
WC1B 3DP

80 Maiden Lane
Suite 704
New York, NY 10038

www.continuumbooks.com

First edition published 2011
Paperback edition published 2012

British Library Cataloguing-in-Publication Data
A catalogue record for this book is available from the British Library.

ISBN: 978-1-4411-8321-7 (hardcover)
978-1-4411-0070-2 (paperback)

Library of Congress Cataloging-in-Publication Data
Education, dialogue and hermeneutics / edited by Paul Fairfield.
p. cm.
Includes bibliographical references.
ISBN: 978-1-4411-8321-7 (hardcover)
1. Education–Philosophy. 2. Education–Research. 3. Communication in education.
4. Hermeneutics. I. Fairfield, Paul, 1966– II. Title.

LB14.7.E392 2010
370.1–dc22 2010016142

Typeset by Newgen Imaging Systems Pvt Ltd, Chennai, India
Printed and bound in Great Britain

For Gwyneth Fairfield

Contents

Notes on Contributors

Babette Babich is professor of philosophy at Fordham University and executive editor of *New Nietzsche Studies.* Her recent works include *Words in Blood, Like Flowers* (2006), *Nietzsche, Habermas, and Critical Theory* (edited volume, 2004), and numerous articles on Nietzsche, Heidegger, and Hölderlin.

Nicholas Davey is professor of philosophy at the University of Dundee. He is the author of *Seeing Otherwise* (forthcoming), *Unquiet Understanding* (2006), and numerous articles on hermeneutics, aesthetics, and Nietzsche.

Paul Fairfield is associate professor of philosophy at Queen's University. His recent books include *Philosophical Hermeneutics Reinterpreted* (2011) and *Education After Dewey* (2009). He is former editor of *Symposium: Canadian Journal of Continental Philosophy.*

Shaun Gallagher is professor of philosophy and cognitive sciences at the University of Central Florida. He is editor of *Phenomenology and the Cognitive Sciences* and author of *Brainstorming* (2008), *Hermeneutics and Education* (1992), and numerous works in the philosophy of mind, phenomenology, and hermeneutics.

Jean Grondin is professor of philosophy at Université de Montréal and adjunct professor at the University of Ottawa. He is the author of several books on hermeneutics, including *Hans-Georg Gadamer: A Biography* (2003) and *Introduction to Philosophical Hermeneutics* (1997).

Graeme Nicholson is professor emeritus of philosophy at the University of Toronto. He has authored numerous works in hermeneutics and ontology, including *Justifying Our Existence* (2009), *Illustrations of Being* (1997), and *Hans-Georg Gadamer on Education, Poetry, and History* (edited volume, 1992).

Ramsey Eric Ramsey is associate professor of social and behavioral sciences at Arizona State University. He is coauthor of *Leaving Us to Wonder* (2005) and author of *The Long Path to Nearness* (1987) and other works in the philosophy of science and communication.

Andrzej Wiercinski is president and founder of the International Institute for Hermeneutics. His edited volumes include *Hermeneutics and the Art of Conversation* (forthcoming), *Phronetic Rationality* (forthcoming), and *Between Suspicion and Sympathy* (2003).

Introduction

Education, Dialogue and Hermeneutics

Paul Fairfield

What is decisive in education may well be the most elusive to reflection. We turn to the theory of education in order to clarify and gain critical perspective on the practice, but when the practical business of teaching and learning is not only complex but exceedingly so, clarity can be far to seek, not least because the matter of which we are speaking is at once tangible and intangible. There are dimensions of education, we commonly believe, that are empirical, technical, and utilitarian. None would contest that in education we are imparting information and skills whose use-value in the world is unquestionable. Teachers are charged with the practical tasks of "covering the material," instilling a curriculum, and preparing students for examinations, perhaps by means of a technique that is efficient and which can be expected to secure measurable outcomes. Rather often, however, educators have upheld an additional view that coexists uneasily with the first. This is that there is more to education than what can be spoken of within an empirical, technical, and utilitarian vocabulary, and perhaps a great deal more. When we are speaking of intangibles, a discourse that is tied too closely to the empirical can miss a good deal of the point of education and compress the whole business into a theoretical model that omits what is decisive. Educators in all disciplines and at all levels require some basic orientation that transcends the immediate business of transmitting knowledge, yet when one turns to the educational literature one finds an array of approaches, methods, and disciplinary vocabularies the relations between which are often as unclear as their relevance for practice. What follows, one might ask, from the latest findings in educational psychology in the real world of education? What difference does it make, one might also ask, whether we are critical theorists, progressives, or poststructuralists in the classroom? The relevance of theory to practice must be evident, but as anyone who has waded into this literature can attest, this is not always the case.

If the implications of educational theory for what actually happens, or might happen, in classrooms are not always clear, a further problem is that a good deal of our theorizing has a narrowing effect on how we think about education. Theoretical reflection in general aims to clarify its object, yet the clarity that we seek must not be purchased at the cost of oversimplification or any reduction in the complexity of the things themselves. When we insist that education, and educational research, be brought within a framework of utility and scientificity we run the risk of misunderstanding through oversimplification. If the practice of education is variable and intangible, at least in part and particularly in its higher reaches, our theorizing must reflect this fact and not insist that the phenomena be made to fit a model imported from the sciences. Without doubt, a good part of education lends itself to quantitative, empirical, and utilitarian analysis, yet a good part of it also does not.

If the thinking that prevails in educational faculties and teachers' colleges is a theoretical hodgepodge, a good deal of it remains beholden to a positivism that in philosophy went into eclipse long ago. It is positivism in a new guise, of course, one that is anxiously concerned with establishing the scientific credentials of education as a discipline in the university. From the point of view of the non-positivist, the preoccupation with disciplinary legitimation can be excessive and cause us to uphold research models that are reductive and scientistic. What we must not lose sight of is that while education has an empirical dimension, the practice itself is neither a science nor a technique but an art. Fundamentally it is an art of leading forth or drawing out (*educere*) of the mind and raising it to some higher condition. Plato's allegory of the cave still has a certain authority here. We are speaking of a process that is not disconnected from ordinary experience and the search for understanding that belongs to it, but that builds upon this in some fashion or other. Like any art, it involves a complex of activities and capacities that resist the reduction to technique and that do not always lend themselves to empirical measure. If we would understand education, we must understand the intangibles of the classroom and the higher purposes that it serves—higher, that is, than the vocational and the pragmatic narrowly conceived. Many educational theorists have made this case before, and in a great variety of ways. One contemporary trend, for instance, speaks of a dialogical dimension of education that goes beyond the straightforward bestowing of information on essentially docile minds—the kind of model often defended by educational conservatives, among others. Education in its higher reaches, many now believe, involves a kind of Socratic back-and-forth between teachers, students, and subject matter, an informal art of conversation that is aimed at liberating young minds from their parochialism and possibly their oppression. Paulo Freire and the movement of critical pedagogy that he inspired take the theme of dialogue in a decidedly political direction, and it is a movement that has had a good deal of influence. Curiously absent from the discussion, however, is the foremost philosopher of dialogue of the last half-century.

Hans-Georg Gadamer's philosophical hermeneutics is an explicitly dialogical philosophy that is rich in implications for the theory and practice of education. If to date these implications have been underanalyzed, this volume endeavors to correct this. The following chapters draw in different ways upon insights from the foremost hermeneutical thinkers of the nineteenth and twentieth centuries, and Gadamer in particular. Among the themes they take up are the meaning of a humanist education, the relevance of hermeneutical dialogue, intersubjective understanding and the acquisition of narrative competence, *Bildung* and exemplarity, self-education and the thinking teacher, the limits of the vocational and utilitarian, and the nature of educational experience.

A hermeneutical theory of education is articulated not at some remove from the practice itself but as a phenomenological description of teaching and learning as they occur within institutions or without them. It is an interpretation of what we do when the process is successful—what aims we have achieved and what has made their achievement possible—and, equally important, what happens to us in the course of our doing—what has transpired behind our back and how we ourselves have been constituted. Education belongs to the larger life process that is the search for understanding of our world and ourselves and is continuous with human experience in general. It is not a special form of activity or technique of which ordinary experience knows nothing, but at the best of times raises such experience to a higher order of explicitness and sophistication. Plato's account of this process was not wholly mistaken; while educators do not altogether know what is true and are not charged with leading students to behold the Forms or their contemporary equivalents, their role involves leading the mind out of its ignorance, narrowness, and self-satisfaction in a process that is difficult and unending. Like Socratic dialogue, the educative process carries us along in a logic of question and answer in which no one has the last word. It forms the soul and leaves us not in secure possession of the truth but in its relentless pursuit.

Perhaps no practice is as vulnerable as education to societal trends, political pressure, and meddling from the well-meaning but uninformed. Likely it has always been so and so it will remain. It falls to educators to resist much of this a good deal of the time and to recall the higher purposes that education serves, however we understand these. Education informs while also forming and transforming students and educators no less. Teachers are not technicians, nor are they experts or facilitators of a certain kind. If education is a transformation or a rising up of some ambiguous kind—from intellectual immaturity to maturity, from narrow horizons to broad ones, or something of the kind—then the educator's role is to lead students in this direction, and in a way that eludes ready description. The educated mind is many things; it is not only informed or credentialed but reflective, open, and unsatisfied with what it imagines it knows. It is able to look up, if not from a Platonic theater of illusion, then from the details and practicalities of life and to seek a broader understanding and self-understanding. It may also possess the kind of intellectual virtues of which hermeneutics speaks. Education can no longer be thought of on the model of a straightforward transfer of information from the one who knows to the many who do not, but must be conceived in a more dialogical and transformative way. The following studies pursue many of the implications of this hypothesis and, it may be hoped, in ways that educators across the disciplines may see the relevance. While this volume makes a contribution to the philosophy of education, our hope is that it will be relevant not only to specialists in this field but to educators in all fields who seek a larger understanding of their practice.

Chapter 1

Gadamer's Experience and Theory of Education: Learning that the Other May Be Right

Jean Grondin

Hans-Georg Gadamer, one of the founders with Paul Ricoeur of modern-day hermeneutics, was not primarily a philosopher of education, but he often wrote on the issue and his philosophy has important consequences for our understanding of the main goals of education.[1] His primary focus in his major work *Truth and Method*, published in 1960, was to develop a "hermeneutical" theory which would do justice to the truth claim of the humanities. But in so doing, he helped us understand what knowledge means for the human sciences and thus what education, in those sciences but also more generally, is all about. Gadamer always said that any good theory must grow out of practice. So it is, one should assume, with his ideas about education. Before we deal with his views on education, it might be appropriate to know something about Gadamer's own upbringing.

The Education of Hans-Georg Gadamer

Gadamer's life spans three centuries: he was born on February 11, 1900, and died on March 13, 2002, at the outset of the twenty-first century. He was the son of a prominent pharmaceutical chemist who wanted, it seems, his son to follow his footsteps and study the rigorous sciences. But, alas, his son would be attracted by the arts, letters, and philosophy, which his father would dismiss as the "bantering sciences." It was a major disappointment for him, all the more so since he was his only son who would pursue university studies (Gadamer's only other sibling, his older brother, suffered from chronic epilepsy which hindered him from pursuing higher studies). Yet, he saw to it that Hans-Georg received a stringent education. In his autobiography, Gadamer described the situation in his home city of

Breslau, Silesia, an Eastern province of Germany (which is now in Poland), as "more Prussian than Prussia."[2] By this, he hints that rigid discipline and military virtues were paramount in his childhood, as was the respect for authority.

Gadamer received his entire elementary and high school education at the same institution, the 400-year-old Holy Spirit Gymnasium in Breslau, where this sense of discipline was all-pervasive, especially during the war years (1914–18). It was a "humanist" school, which means that he learned languages like French, Latin, and Greek, and through a most rigorous learning process; when he studied French, for instance, he would spend an entire year just learning the right phonetic pronunciation of French words before learning their meanings.[3] He ended up with a perfect pronunciation, but no child today would endure such torture. In the Latin and Greek classes, his teachers would of course extol the military examples of the "classics." As a child, Gadamer was quite taken by this military Prussian tradition and served in a small corps for children. One even predicted that he would follow the career of a military officer.[4] This military idealism was however shattered to pieces by the experience of the First World War. When it started, he was only 14, and was replete with nationalistic sentiment, but avoided service, at the beginning because he was too young, and later because he suffered from malnourishment as a consequence of the catastrophic supply situation in Germany. Germany suffered a humiliating defeat. In education, Gadamer would later often stress, it is important to learn to lose and at an early age. It helps one to become aware of one's limits and remain open to other points of view (a crucial point, as we will see, for Gadamer's philosophy of education).

In 1918 the ideology of Prussian Germany, in which he was raised, also received a trouncing: the absurd trench warfare between the most "civilized" nations on Earth, which had slaughtered millions to no end, devastated the ideology of progress according to which science and industry would lead to a world of peace and prosperity. Indeed, for him, it was the entire tradition of Western Enlightenment which suffered a blow. In the aftermath of the war, the 18-year-old Gadamer, disillusioned by the ideology of scientific progress, was understandably more attracted by the world of poetry, theater, and literature. He was quite impressed by a German teacher at his Gymnasium, Hermann Reichert, who devoted himself with rigor and discipline to his literary studies, in spite of the ongoing war. It was a decisive example for him because he would later often claim that the main function of school is to provide one with a model which one can follow and which would decide one's career: in education, he would always stress, programs are less important than this finding of a model. At the time Gadamer was also enthralled by the poetry and worldview of Stefan George and his "circle." It was a movement with pedagogical implications since it defended the view that the poet, and Stefan George himself, was a leading figure in the education of Germany. His circle was quite an elitist lot, which looked down with disdain on modern mathematical science and the vulgarity of everyday life. In his autobiography of 1977, Gadamer still praised the "value tables of the George circle" which "represented in an increasingly atomistic society a corporative consciousness of high spiritual voltage which attracted him and whose determination and assurance he could not but admire."[5] Gadamer did not really become a member of the George circle, but remained close to some of its members throughout the course of his studies.

With those influences, and as a kind of rebellion against the pressure he felt from his father, it was clear that he would devote himself to literature, the arts, and philosophy. Philosophy finally won out, because it was the spirit of the arts and literature that attracted him, not the formal, scholarly aspects of those disciplines. He had the good fortune of studying with some of the best thinkers of his time, most notably Martin Heidegger, Nicolai Hartman, Paul Natorp, Richard Hönigswald, Ernst Robert Curtius, Rudolf Bultmann, and some of the finest humanists in ancient philology, such as Paul Friedländer and Werner Jaeger, who was famous, among other things, for his work on Greek humanism and its paradigmatic importance for education (an idea he defended in his book *Paideia*). He knew them during the course of his studies at the University of Breslau (1918–19), but mostly at the University of Marburg (1919–28). The climate of the idyllic university town of Marburg was perhaps as significant as the ideas that he absorbed. The German university system, especially before the "*Massenuniversität*" which sprang up in the 1960s, was not very standardized or "school-like" ("*verschult*," as they say in German), that is, based on credits, numerous exams, and the like. It was rather small, reserved for the chosen few, and it encouraged experiment (a vital term for Gadamer). One embarked on university studies as on an adventure, studying a vast array of disciplines (Gadamer attended lectures in literature, art history, philosophy, ancient philology, history, even Sanskrit, and some theology, in short, whatever was interesting) and with time one gained close contact with an important teacher, of whom one would become the pupil. This type of education often became very personal. For instance, Gadamer met his most influential teacher, Martin Heidegger, already a well-known figure, during the fall semester at the University of Freiburg in 1923, and in the following summer, Heidegger would invite Gadamer and his wife to spend four weeks at his private hut in the Black Forest and hold private seminars on Aristotle with him. This form of teaching was by no means exceptional in the old German university: aside from their formal teaching duties, all university professors would form private reading and discussion groups to which they would invite their most gifted students. Gadamer took part in many such groups, where he surely learned more than in the classes (learning, he would restate in 1999, does not only come from the teachers, but also from the class mates), and would himself form such circles when he would become a professor.[6]

In short, if Gadamer's first instruction in the Breslau school was austere, his university education, after the earth-shattering event of the First World War, was far more personal, unconstrained, and based on direct contact with the teacher. But the standards were by no means relaxed, quite on the contrary. Gadamer studied for some years as the pupil of Heidegger, but his teacher grew somewhat disillusioned with him. In a cool letter he penned to him on February 14, 1925, Heidegger warned him "that if you don't become hard enough with yourself and get down to hard work, then you are making yourself illusions about what awaits you in a serious academic career."[7] Gadamer was shaken but took good heed of Heidegger's advice: he decided to change his ways and embark on a demanding three-year education program in Greek philology (which led to a "state exam"). He did this, one should note, at the age of 25 after he had received his doctorate in 1922, at the tender age of 22. The German Ph.D. was not as elaborate at the time as it is today: it was more akin to what one would nowadays call an M.A. thesis, but it enabled one to snatch a "*Doktor*" title, which carries a special weight in Germany where academics use their degrees. In a sense, the real studies began after the doctorate. The important degree for an academic was the "habilitation," which Gadamer received in 1928, with a more earnest thesis. It marked the end of his studies and the beginning of a teaching career as a (shoddily paid) "*Privatdozent*," who had to earn a name for himself in the hope of receiving a regular professorship in the coming years (which would prove quite taxing, to say the least). But Gadamer also learned other life lessons immediately after his 1922 doctorate: he was stricken with a severe polio infection which left him somewhat crippled for the rest of his life. It taught him that a major illness early in life is an important asset: one learns to practice moderation in taking care of one's health (it must have worked, since he lived to be 102). After his habilitation, by Heidegger, in 1928, Gadamer remained a devoted teacher for the rest of his life. He struggled along as a *Privatdozent* in Marburg from 1929 to 1938, before he became a full-fledged university professor in Leipzig in 1939, where he was named rector after the war (1946–7), in large part because he had not compromised himself with the Nazis and never became a party member. Seeing, however, that the imposition of a new ideological straightjacket was inexorable in the East, he left Leipzig, in the Eastern part of Germany, for Frankfurt in 1947, before he became the successor of Karl Jaspers in Heidelberg in 1949. His book *Truth and Method* (1960) earned him growing fame and wide international recognition. But he was such a passionate teacher that he continued to teach well beyond his retirement (*Emeritierung*) in 1968, not only at his university of Heidelberg, but also at foreign universities in Europe and North America where he was invited, well into his late nineties. All the while, Gadamer kept in close contact with his many students in Germany and around the world, thus underscoring that education was a personal and lifelong encounter.

Gadamer's Vibrant Humanism: Learning from the Classics

Until *Truth and Method* appeared in 1960, when he was already sixty, Gadamer had published very little (quality still trumped quantity in those happy days). The book was indeed his first major book publication since his habilitation on Plato appeared in 1931. To be sure, the Nazi era, during which Gadamer remained quiet and did not compromise himself (unlike his teacher Heidegger), was not conducive to publications. But Gadamer first understood himself as someone who always had something to learn and it is this humanist sense of constant learning that he conveyed to his students in Marburg, Leipzig, Frankfurt, Heidelberg, and at many foreign universities. Since 1936, he regularly gave lectures conceived as an "Introduction to the Human Sciences," where he taught that it was basically in the field of history, the arts, and the humanities that one would encounter the basic truths about human nature. His teaching, and his own learning process, took on the form of an ongoing dialogue with the classics in philosophy and the humanities. His students were quite impressed by his teaching and pressed Gadamer to publish his ideas on the subject. It is thus that *Truth and Method* came to be.

The book first offered what it called a "hermeneutics." The term sounded strange at the time, but if it later became something like a household name it is largely due to Gadamer's pioneering work. The word was certainly familiar to theologians, since hermeneutics was the discipline that provided rules for the correct interpretation of sacred texts. But the German philosopher Wilhelm Dilthey (1833–1911) began using the term in conjunction with his aim of justifying the truth claim of the humanities (*Geisteswissenschaften*). This claim had become a puzzle in light of the successes of the exact sciences in the nineteenth century. Physics and mathematics are sciences, to be sure, but to what extent can that be said of literature, history, and even philosophy? The triumph of the exact sciences surely had something to do with the stringency of their methods, it was believed, so all the human sciences needed to do to "catch up," as it were, was to ascertain their own methods to garner truth and thus scientific respectability. For Dilthey, the methods of the natural sciences were viewed as methods of *explaining* (*Erklären*), say, an occurrence out of a universal law, whereas the humanities had to provide rules for *understanding* (*Verstehen*), that is, sorting out the interior meaning of a phenomenon of "spiritual" value through its expression, for instance, what an author wanted to convey in a poem or what a historical monument meant. First and foremost, these guidelines for understanding would enable one to contain the subjectivity and prejudices of the interpreter and thus guarantee some kind of objectivity. As in the exact sciences, even if the methods were different for each field, it was the independence of the results from the observer that would vouch for verifiability and thus scientificity.

It was this entire conception of knowledge, and of education, in the humanities, that Gadamer called into question. Is truth in the human sciences really something independent from the knower? Can the distance toward the object function as the right model if one wishes to understand the humanities and the task of education more generally? Gadamer believed that a foreign ideal was here being impressed on the humanities. It had undeniable success in the exact sciences and was thus most attractive, but it failed to do justice to what education is all about. Education, Gadamer argued, is about "formation" (*Bildung*), so the individual who is being formed or educated is implicated in the process from the outset (to shut him out would be to miss the point of education altogether). The education of the individual is achieved through the engagement with works of art, culture, science, and history. It is through this encounter, which is always the beginning of a dialogue with them, that one learns to develop one's thinking and outlook on life. This conviction was for Gadamer the main idea of humanism, that is, that one can learn from the classics and history, all the more since all our understanding is framed by them. It is Gadamer's stated purpose to justify the truth claim of the humanities and the aim of education out of the main tenets of humanism, which the methodical ideal, borrowed from the exact sciences, had somewhat relegated into oblivion in the last two centuries.[8] Indeed, Gadamer's most important contribution to the study of education lies in his retrieval of the humanist tradition of education at the beginning of *Truth and Method*.

It is a tradition Gadamer revives by relying on thinkers such as Herder and Hegel, but also the Napolitan humanist Giambattista Vico and the seventeenth-century Spanish essayist Balthasar Gracian. Their basic conviction is that the human being is a being in need of "*Bildung*," that is, of education and forming. In the words of Herder, one needs to "rise up to humanity through culture."[9] There is a slightly metaphysical reason for this, for Herder and Hegel: unlike the other animals, man is not endowed through instinct with his basic abilities, but is characterized by the break with the immediate and the natural. "He is not by nature what he should be."[10] He thus has to cultivate his rational abilities and rise to a certain "universality": he needs to learn to see things in a broader perspective. *Bildung* chiefly happens through this broadening of one's own horizons: to educate oneself means to incorporate as many different points of view as one can and thus to elevate oneself above one's own particularity and learn to view it with some perspective. This goes hand in hand with a "receptivity to the otherness" of a work of art or of the past. This is crucial since it sums up in a nutshell Gadamer's view on education: "That is what, following Hegel, we emphasized as the general characteristic of *Bildung* [education, formation]: keeping oneself open to what is other—*to other more universal points of view*. It embraces a sense of moderation and distance in relation to itself, and hence consists in raising above itself to universality. To distance oneself from oneself and from one's own private purposes means *to look at these in the way others see them*. This universality is by no means a universality of the concept or understanding. This is not the case of a particular being deduced from a universal; nothing is proved conclusively. The universal viewpoints to which the cultivated man keeps himself open are not a fixed applicable yardstick, but are present to him only as the viewpoints of possible others. Thus the cultivated consciousness has in fact more the character of a *sense*."[11]

Education gives us a "sense" of other viewpoints, ever more perspectives, and of our particularity. As Gadamer would later say, the soul of his hermeneutics lies in the recognition "that the other might be right."[12] It goes hand in hand with a sense of one's own modesty. An educated person is not one who can display an impressive repertoire of certainties one has gained here and there; it is a person who is aware of one's own ignorance. Those who like to show off their knowledge are called "pedants," and they are not the models of the cultivated individual for Gadamer. A person with culture will rather adopt a position of detachment, a distance toward the knowledge that characterizes the pedant. Gadamer said it beautifully in a lecture on the purpose of a "general education" (*allgemeine Bildung*) he gave in 1995: "To be cultured is obviously to cultivate a particular form of distance. Hegel already wondered what constituted a cultured person. The cultured person is the one who is ready to admit as plausible (literally, to value) the thoughts of others. Here, one discovers at the same time a remarkable description of the uncultured person: it is typically the person who maintains in all possible circumstances and in all possible situations and with a dictatorial assurance whatever wisdom he has picked up by happenstance. On the contrary, to leave something undecided is what constitutes the essence of those who can ask questions. The person who does not recognize one's own ignorance and, for that reason, acknowledge the open character of some decisions, and precisely in order to find the right solution, will never be what is called a cultured person. The cultured person is not the one who displays superior knowledge, but only the one who, to take an expression from Socrates, has not forgotten the knowledge of his ignorance."[13]

How can one describe this type of knowledge? Gadamer refers here to the notion of "sense" since it is not something that is the consequence of a demonstration, known by reasons alone, or that one could learn from textbooks like a mathematical formula. It has something of a "common sense," a sense of what is shared and makes our humanity possible, what is also called in French the "*bon sens*," the nurturing of which is the task of education.

Gadamer retrieves here the pivotal humanist notion of *sensus communis*, which modern science had discredited because it did not correspond to its ideal of a knowledge of (mathematical) reasons. Originally, the *sensus communis* was viewed as the common root of the five senses which put us in contact with the outside world.[14] It is a special sense since it has to *combine* what is transmitted through the senses. It goes beyond what is immediately given and forms a kind of independent judgment on things. Authors like Vico viewed it as a sense of what is right and what is good, also a sense of the common good, which can only be cultivated since it cannot be learned. It is at the same time a *bon sens*, a "good sense" (a sense of the good and which it is good to have), and a *common* sense, a sense of what is common and thus grounds our humanity. In *Truth and Method*, Gadamer recalls that the humanists understood very well that this sense, which they compared to a kind of tact or "taste" for what is right, was not provided by science alone. Science has to do with what is certain and demonstrable. *Sensus communis* has more to do with what is probable (*verisimile*), what is likely and fair, which encompasses the most important part of our ethical and political lives. This is why they drew a sharp distinction between the scholar and the wise man, which parallels the distinction between *sophia* (science) and *phronesis* (prudence).[15] The aim of a humanist education is not to build "scientists" but wise and prudent persons, who will also be aware of the limits of science. But how can this sense be cultivated? There is no mathematical formula, but some clues offer an idea of how this can be done or attempted.

A Culture of Questioning

The educational ideal circumscribed by the notions of *Bildung* and *sensus communis* provides one less with answers than with open questions. To be sure, there are a lot of answers being offered to all sorts of problems, also in the field of education, but for Gadamer, the hallmark of a humanist education is to enable one to raise the right type of questions. He finds his model in Socrates. His only, yet precious wisdom lay in the fact that he knew he did not know anything for certain. He asked those who pretended to be "learned" what was the good, but never received a satisfying answer. His discipline, and superiority, was one of questioning. A person with education (*Bildung*) is one with a broad horizon, who has integrated various perspectives, and knows how to leave things in the open, as Gadamer likes to say. It is through *Bildung* that we become aware that others think differently and, lest we forget, that "others after us will also understand in a different way."[16] No way of seeing things is definitive and no one sees everything. Hence, true education and *Bildung* reside in the ability to question acquired knowledge in order to open up new perspectives. It allows us, says Gadamer, to "gain horizon" (*Horizont gewinnen*) or to learn to put things in perspective. What one puts into perspective is one's own viewpoint as well as those whom one comes across in the dialogue with the tradition which is another name for the educative process. It allows one to gain distance and to distrust too easy answers: "The concept of 'horizon' suggests itself because it expresses the superior breadth of vision that the person who is trying to understand must have. To acquire a horizon means that one learns to look beyond what is close at hand—not in order to look away from it but to see it better, within a larger whole and in truer proportion."[17]

To acquire a horizon, that is, education, means to learn to raise questions. "A true question," Gadamer would always emphasize, "is a question to which one does not know the answer." The so-called pedagogical or rhetorical question to which the teacher knows the answer is for Gadamer not a real question.[18] Learning to raise questions, new questions, develops the imagination and the faculty of judgment, whereas the learning of answers only cultivates the memory. What education should stimulate and value most highly is this capacity of judgment, which is another name for human freedom. This is why Gadamer praises risk-taking by the individual, audacity, the courage (*Wagemut*) to venture new ideas.[19] This is the only way one can learn, since one can then learn to think for oneself. If one errs, one will find out soon enough, through trial and error, and garner experience, which one never acquires if one never takes risks.

Gadamer himself was known in his oral exams as a university professor to ask the candidates questions to which he himself did not know the answer. It was less important for him to see if someone had learned something by heart (everybody can do that) than to discover how one would deal with an open question. He was convinced that "in an exam, one should give higher worth to a false answer which is defended correctly than to a right answer [which is not]."[20] Otherwise what is promoted in education is only conformity and adaptation to what already is.[21] Education is about something else: it is about being able to form an independent judgment about things. It is for Gadamer the consequence of a culture of questioning.

Education as a Fusion of Horizons

The encounter with tradition, which is education, as we have just seen, calls us into question.[22] It is not just some content that has to be learned, according to the "conformist" model of education. On the contrary, one has to hear in tradition a voice that challenges us and elicits our reaction and judgment. This is why Gadamer famously describes the encounter with tradition, and thereby the process of learning, as a "fusion of horizons."[23] It is a crucial notion, indeed one of the most decisive in Gadamer's hermeneutics and educational outlook. The fusion operates on many levels.

First, there is the fusion between the knower (say, the *interpretans*) and what he or she is learning (the *interpretandum*), between the pupil and the object of her learning. One is first taken up, challenged by what is said. That only occurs if what is said speaks to us and our present (it certainly helps in this regard if the teacher, who is in the best of cases a model, is taken up by what he or she is teaching). Interpretation and education thus take on the form of a *dialogue* between the learning pupil and its subject matter, in the case of historical knowledge between the past and the present. What is learned is thus incorporated into our view of things, both, it must be emphasized, in its similarity (it has something to say in which we can *recognize* ourselves and know ourselves better) and its difference (it is *another* view of things which expands our perspective, our horizon).

In order to attend this difference, Gadamer also specifically urges a "controlled" fusion of horizons.[24] To be sure, we tend to absorb what is transmitted to us from the past, unknowingly applying to it our own perspectives, but we need to become aware of its otherness and thus of our very own. For this, it is incumbent upon us to reflect upon the way the past has been transmitted to us. What is transmitted is part of the present, yet different: it allows us to take into account the difference of the past and of the present itself. In Gadamer's terms, we need to become aware of the "effective history" (*Wirkungsgeschichte*) at work in our understanding. We never understand at a zero point of history, but engage in a dialogue that has started before us. This effective history is not something we can ever master once and for all—according to Gadamer we belong far more to history than it belongs to us—but this historical "limitation" has an upshot: it will lead us to more openness to what is foreign.

Gadamer's fusion of horizons further means that what is learned must be *translated* and thus "applied" to the present. Application (*Anwendung, applicatio*) forms a key part of Gadamer's notion of understanding. To understand is not only to swallow, as it were, an intellectual meaning, it is a "grasping" in which we are also the ones who are "grasped," by what is at stake. This only happens if we are able to translate in our own words what it is we understand. We only understand, Gadamer contends, to the extent that we search and find words for what we strive to understand.

The fusion of horizons Gadamer is ultimately hinting at is the fusion that takes place between understanding and its linguistic formulation. Language is for Gadamer the unsurpassable medium of our understanding: whatever we understand can be put into words, and that which we do not understand is that for which we have found no words yet. Language is not to be viewed as a limit or a prison for understanding: it is able to search and find expression for everything that can be understood. Hence the "fundamental priority of language" for Gadamer's hermeneutics: there is no understanding without it.[25]

Obvious conclusions follow from this for the task of education. It will bestow utmost importance on historical knowledge, language, and literature, so that one can learn more properly one's own history and language, a never-ending task, but also on the learning of foreign languages since they bring us into contact with other worldviews, ways of saying and understanding which can only broaden our horizons.

It is worth noting in this regard that Charles Taylor recently heralded Gadamer's idea of a fusion of horizons as the most adequate model for the understanding of foreign cultures, which is a growing task, and challenge, in this age of globalization. When we strive to understand other cultures, we cannot do so assuming our culture is superior. Gadamer teaches us, according to Taylor, that "really taking in the other will involve an identity shift in us": there is "no understanding the other without a changed understanding of self."[26] Learning to know other cultures and ways of thinking surely changes the view we have of our own culture: it has, to be sure, an "identity cost," in that it makes us discover the provinciality of our own perspective, but we are also enriched by it in that it helps us to realize "what other possibilities there are in our world."[27] Following the idea of a fusion of horizons, understanding (*Verstehen*) appears less like a scientific grasp of an object than as a coming to an understanding with someone, and even with oneself.[28] It is in this coming to an understanding that culture unfolds.

The Meaning of Culture

What we acquire in the encounter with tradition is a sense of culture. But culture starts with oneself. It is a "*cultura sui*" or "*cultura animi*," a culture of the soul in the Ciceronian sense. It means that one should "cultivate" one's own self like one cultivates a garden or a soil, that is, one ploughs it, turning it up in all directions, removing the rocks and debris that impede growth, in order to plant seeds that will hopefully bear fruit.[29] One too easily forgets this original sense of culture, in the singular, when one speaks nowadays of the different "cultures" of the world. There is this plurality, of course, but it means that there are different ways of cultivating the soul and thus of educating oneself. The more we can take into account, the better, since this allows us to discover and appreciate the diversity of what it means to be human.

What is transmitted and what is learned through education is culture. "Culture" can be understood, Gadamer states, "*als der Bereich all dessen, was dadurch mehr wird, daß wir es teilen*," "as the domain of all that which becomes more by virtue of the fact that we share it."[30] It is the sum of that which helps us "build" ourselves to become better human beings. "Culture," he adds, "is that which might hinder the humans from attacking one another and to become worse than any animal," since animals do not have any equivalent for human wars.[31] Wars are not started because of different cultures, they break out because of a *lack* of culture, that is, the capacity to view oneself with the eyes of the other and thus to put into perspective one's own point of view.

The hope of education is to bring about this sense of culture, this distancing from oneself and broadening of one's own horizons. In this regard, it is also helpful, Gadamer reminds us, to attend to what is *common* to all cultures and what constitutes our humanity. We live in a world of differences, where the non-identical, the conflicts and the oppositions are often stressed. But this should not hide the fact that these differences only exist against the backdrop of a common humanity, to which true culture should also educate us: "It seems to me to be a shortcoming in our public sphere that what is raised to our consciousness is only the different, the controversial, the disputable and the dubious and that what is common and binding remains without a voice. We are perhaps harvesting the fruit of a too long education for the different and a sensibility that calls for the taking into account of the differences. Our historical education goes in that direction and our political customs have let the oppositions and the fighting attitude become the overriding evidence. Here, a reflection on the more profound solidarities in all aspects of human life might be advantageous. We have to rediscover what has become a social task in light of the decreasing binding force of the churches and of religion: to elevate to consciousness that which unites us."[32] What unites us is that we are beings in need of constant education, who can only learn from one another, especially in an ever more global universe. We thus partake in a dialogue that has gone on before us and that will continue long after us, and in which we are less the masters than the participants.

Education is Self-Education

For Gadamer, education is not a process that comes to a close once and for all, nor is it one which is confined to the school. One never stops to learn, and this means to educate oneself and to remain open to other perspectives. At the age of 99, Gadamer was invited to give a talk in a Gymnasium in Bremen, as he often was (he was still giving lectures to young pupils when he was 101), and he began by almost excusing himself for having to give a formal talk, since he would find it more interesting to conduct a dialogue and learn from the participants what *their* thoughts about education were all about: "I am a feeble old man and you must not therefore expect that I am now at the height of my productivity or even my wisdom. In any case it is somewhat dubious to claim to be at the height of one's wisdom. For all that, when one is such an old man, one can undoubtedly say: I have accumulated a great deal of experience. But in truth, my attitude towards you is really strange, as I would really like to learn so much from you. I would need to know how things stand with school today, what are the concerns of present-day parents, what concerns your sons and daughters have, and all of that which I no longer know. I have doubted whether I can feel qualified to speak about it. We have already agreed, otherwise I would prescribe it, that we hold a short discussion, so that I do not detain you too long as an audience."[33] There is less coquetry and false modesty than one would assume in this address by a wise old man. This is how Gadamer was: how could a 99-year-old claim to know about the daily problems of present-day education? He did not pretend to know better and would have wanted most of all to learn it from those concerned, the pupils, the teachers, and the parents. This is why he kept stressing that education is always self-education: it is not something that goes from the parents or the teachers "downwards" to the pupil. It starts with the pupil that we never cease to be. It has to do with our quest to become at home in this world, "*Sicheinhausen*," which is never-ending in this changing world of ours.[34] We are thrown into this existence and the first thing we must learn is to live with others. One cannot learn to live with others if one thinks one is always right. This is why one of the important lessons of life is to learn to lose, so that we can accept that others often have a better hold on things, from which we can only learn. The way of reason is not to think one is right and to try to defend one's views with unbending arguments; it is to acknowledge that the other might be right. Indeed: "The one who speaks in the name of reason contradicts himself. To be reasonable is to be aware of the limitation of one's own insight and thus to become capable of better insight, wherever it may come."[35]

Notes

[1] Most notably in his *opus magnum*, *Truth and Method*. But the issue of education is one Gadamer dealt with throughout his career. One of his earliest essays was titled "Plato's State of Education," published in 1942 ("*Platos Staat der Erziehung*" in *Das neue Bild der Antike*, edited by Helmut Berve, Leipzig: Koehler & Amelang, I. Band: Hellas, 1942, 317–33; now in his *Complete Works Edition*: *Gesammelte Werke*, vol. 5, Tübingen: Mohr Siebeck, 1985, 249–62) and one of his latest book publications was a short lecture he gave in 1999 and that was published under the title "Education is Self-Education," translated by J. Cleary and P. Hogan, in *Journal of Philosophy of Education* 35 (2001), 529–38 (*Erziehung ist sich erziehen*,

Heidelberg, 2000). See also the informative collection *Hans-Georg Gadamer on Education, Poetry, and History*, edited by D. Misgeld and G, Nicholson, Albany: SUNY Press, 1992.

2 Hans-Georg Gadamer, *Philosophische Lehrjahre* (Frankfurt a.M.: Klostermann, 1977), 9. On Gadamer's life and education, see my *Hans-Georg Gadamer: A Biography* (New Haven: Yale University Press, 2003).

3 Gadamer, "Education is Self-Education," 534.

4 Gadamer, *Philosophische Lehrjahre*, 8.

5 Ibid., 17.

6 Gadamer, "Education is Self-Education," 531.

7 Letter of Martin Heidegger to Hans-Georg Gadamer, published in the *Jahresgabe der Martin-Heidegger-Gesellschaft*, 2005/2006, 28.

8 See my "Gadamer on Humanism," in L. E. Hahn, ed., *The Philosophy of Hans-Georg Gadamer*, The Library of Living Philosophers vol. XXIV (Peru, IL.: Open Court Publishing, 1997), 157–70.

9 Gadamer, *Truth and Method*, trans. Joel Weinsheimer and Donald G. Marshall, 2nd rev. ed. (New York: Continuum, 1996), 10; German original in *Wahrheit und Methode, Gesammelte Werke*, vol. 1 (Tübingen: Mohr Siebeck, 1986), 15.

10 Ibid., 12; German original, 17.

11 Ibid., 17 (modified translation, and my emphasis); German original, 22–3.

12 Gadamer, *Über die Verborgenheit der Gesundheit* (Frankfurt a. M.: Suhrkamp, 1993), 109.

13 Lecture given by Gadamer in Heidelberg on July 7, 1995, under the title "What is General Formation today?" (*Was ist allgemeine Bildung heute?*).

14 *Truth and Method*, 22; German original, 27.

15 *Truth and Method*, 20; German original, 25.

16 *Truth and Method*, 373; German original, 379.

17 *Truth and Method*, 305; German original, 310: "*Der Begriff 'Horizont' bietet sich hier an, weil er der übelegenen Weitsicht Ausdruck gibt, die der Verstehende haben muß. Horizont gewinnen meint immer, dass man über das Nahe und Allzunahe hinaussehen lernt, nicht um von ihm wegzusehen, sondern um es in einem grösseren Ganzen und in richtigeren Maßen besser zu sehen.*"

18 See Gadamer, "*Humanismus heute?*," *Humanistische Bildung* 15 (1992), 67: "*Es gehört zum wirklichen Lernen Wagemut. Es gehört dazu, Fragen stellen zu können. Der Mut zum Fragen ist in unserem Erziehungs- und Unterrichtssystem durch die Lehrpläne blockiert. Nun ist die Erziehung zum richtigen Fragen sicherlich außerordentlich schwer. Was ist denn eine Frage? Da würde ich als erstes sagen, eine Frage ist niemals eine solche, auf die man eine Antwort weiß. Die sogenannte pädagogische Frage ist keine echte Frage, die Examensfrage ist eine geradezu lächerliche Form von Scheinfragen. Der Professor fragt etwas, obwohl er die Antwort weiß. Das ist doch keine Frage.*"

19 "Education is Self-Education," 537; "*Humanismus heute?*", 67.

20 "*Humanismus heute?*" (1992), 69: "*Wir brauchen eine neue Sanktion der Urteilskraft. In einem Examen sollte die Antwort, die falsch ist, wenn man sie richtig zu verteidigen weiß, höher gewertet werden als eine richtige Antwort.*"

21 Ibid., 69: "*Darauf kommt es an, daß man auf Fragen mit Denken zu antworten weiß. Das mag ja schön klingen, aber es hat massive Folgen, daß wir nicht so sehr die Anpassung prämieren sollten als die Urteilskraft.*"

22 *Truth and Method*, 374; German original, 379.

23 See my "La fusion des horizons. La version gadamérienne de l'*adaequatio rei et intellectus?*," in *Archives de philosophie* 68 (2005), 401–18.

24 *Truth and Method*, 307; German original, 312.

25 *Truth and Method*, 401; German original, 405.

26 Charles Taylor, "Gadamer on the Human Sciences," in R. Dostal, ed., *The Cambridge Companion to Gadamer* (Cambridge: Cambridge University Press, 2002), 141.

27 Ibid., 141.

28 Ibid., 126.

29 Cicero, *Tusculanae Disputationes*, II. 10 : "*Atque, ut in eodem simili verser, ut ager quamvis fertilis sine cultura fructuosus esse non potest, sic sine doctrina animus; ita est utraque res sine altera debilis. Cultura autem animi philosophia est; haec extrahit vitia radicitus et praeparat animos ad satus accipiendos eaque mandat eis et, ut ita dicam, serit, quae adulta fructus uberrimos ferant.*" See on this sense of culture H.-I. Marrou, *Saint Augustin et la fin de la culture antique* (Paris, éditions De Boccard, 1937), 1983.

[30] Gadamer, "*Die Kultur und das Wort*," in *Lob der Theorie* (Frankfurt a. M.: Suhrkamp, 1983), 15.

[31] Ibid., 19: "*Kultur ist das, was die Menschen daran zu hindern vermag, übereinander herzufallen und schlimmer zu sein als irgendein Tier.*"

[32] Gadamer, *Das Erbe Europas* (Frankfurt a. M.: Suhrkamp, 1989), 156: "*Es scheint mir ein Mangel in unserem öffentlichen Wesen gelegen, daß immer das Differente, das Umstrittene, das Umkämpfte und Bezweifelte in das Bewußtsein der Menschen gehoben wird und daß das wahrhaft Gemeinsame und alle Verbindende sozusagen stimmlos bleibt. Wir ernten wohl die Frucht einer langen Erziehung für das Differente und die Sensibilität, die die Wahrnehmung der Unterschiede verlangt. Unsere historische Erziehung geht in diese Richtung, unsere politische Gewöhnung läßt uns die Gegensätze und die kämpferische Einstellung zur Selbstverständlichkeit werden. Hier könnte, wie mir scheint, eine Besinnung auf die tieferliegenden Solidaritäten in allen Maßstäben des menschlichen Lebens von Gewinn sein. Wir müssen nachholen, was uns seit ein paar Jahrhunderten angesichts des Abnehmens der Bindekraft der Kirchen, der Religion, zu einer gesellschaftlichen Aufgabe geworden ist: das in unser Bewußtsein zu heben, was uns vereint.*"

[33] "Education is Self-Education," 529.

[34] Ibid., 530.

[35] Gadamer, *Lob der Theorie*, 65: "*Wer im Namen der Vernunft spricht, widerspricht sich selbst. Denn vernünftig ist es, die Begrenztheit der eigenen Einsicht zu wissen und eben dadurch besserer Einsicht fähig zu sein, komme sie, woher immer.*"

Chapter 2

Narrative Competence and the Massive Hermeneutical Background

Shaun Gallagher

Children come into formal educational settings already possessing a massive amount of background knowledge and know-how about how the physical world works and about how other people behave. Most of this knowledge is implicit. For purposes of successful educational practice, it is important to have a good understanding of what this background knowledge is and how it informs more explicit cognitive processes. I focus in this chapter on the kind of background knowledge or know-how that enters into intersubjective processes involved in understanding other people.[1]

In the field of hermeneutics the topic under discussion in this chapter is referred to as intersubjective understanding or simply the understanding of others. In different contexts and disciplines such as philosophy of mind, psychology, and the cognitive sciences, this general area of research is referred to as social cognition or theory of mind. I shall begin with a brief review of theories that fit under the heading "theory of mind," and I shall focus on a specific problem that they share, which I call the "starting problem." The solution to this problem, I suggest, requires an alternative way of looking at issues concerning intersubjective understanding and background knowledge.

Theory of Mind

The two standard accounts of how we understand other people are known as the "theory theory" of mind (TT) and simulation theory (ST). These theories have been developed in philosophy of mind and psychology, and more recently have guided research in social neuroscience. They are generally referred to under the heading "theory of mind" (ToM).

TT contends that our everyday way of understanding others is based on folk psychology, a common-sense set of rules, principles, or platitudes that explain how people normally behave. We use folk psychology to infer or "mindread" the other person's beliefs and desires, which in turn explain their behaviors. ST, in contrast, contends that we do not need a theory because we can use our own mind as a model to simulate what must be going on in the other person's mind. We simply put ourselves in their shoes, imagine what we would think, and then project our pretend beliefs and desires into the other's mind.

Both of these approaches share a number of problems[2], but one of the most difficult problems comes at the very beginning of the mindreading process. Neither theory has a good explanation of how the process gets off the ground—or more precisely, what ground we stand on as we engage in the process. For example, the theory theorist will claim that we simply apply our folk-psychological theory by appealing to some specific rule that will explain the other person's behavior. But that seems to assume that we already know what the appropriate rule is for the specific situation. For example, as I drive down the road I see my neighbor raise his hand as I approach. I somehow interpret this as a wave of hello from someone I know. My neighbor *wants* to say hello. I wave back. In another case, however, as I drive down the road I see a police officer hold up her hand. I know that if I simply waved back I would likely get a traffic ticket since it is quite apparent that she *wants* me to stop and *believes* that waving her hand will signal that I should stop. How do I know which rule to apply to interpret this signal? After all, the rules of folk psychology are rather abstract; they supposedly apply to human behavior in general, and, in part, that is what makes them theoretical. The application of such rules may be especially troublesome in ambiguous situations, for example, when my neighbor is the police officer. Does she want to say hello, or does she want me to stop? The issue is this: faced with a particular situation, how do we know which rule to apply?

The situation is no easier for the simulationist. One can see this, for example, in Alvin Goldman's description of the steps involved in running a simulation routine: "First, the attributor creates in herself pretend states intended to match those of the target. In other words, the attributor attempts to put herself in the target's 'mental shoes.' The second step is to feed these initial pretend states [e.g., beliefs] into some mechanism of the attributor's own psychology . . . and allow that mechanism to operate on the pretend states so as to generate one or more new states [e.g., decisions]. Third, the attributor assigns the output state to the target . . . [e.g., we infer or project the decision to the other's mind]."[3] The first step seems tricky. How do I know which pretend state (belief or desire) matches what the other person has in mind? Indeed, is this not what simulation is supposed to explain? If I already knew what state matched the target, then the problem, as defined by ST, would already be solved.

Starting the process seems to be a problem for both TT and ST. Let us call this the *starting problem.* To address this problem some theorists have pursued a hybrid version of theory of mind, that is, a combination of TT and ST. For example, I am in a position to take the first step in the simulation process precisely because I already have a folk psychology that allows me to make a supposition about what the other person is thinking. Theory helps me to get my simulation off the ground. Or perhaps I know what rule of folk psychology to apply because I begin by simulating the other person's situation. It seems to me, however, that these hybrid approaches simply push the problem back a step; one ends up in a questionable circle that turns from abstract rules to unsure suppositions and then returns to abstract rules. This circle, I will argue, is not hermeneutical, precisely because, at least in terms of the TT or ST accounts, it seemingly lacks the right kind of particularistic or contextual knowledge that would be the ground for getting it off the ground.

To be clear, I am not suggesting that theorists of TT and ST would deny that both folk psychology and simulation depend on what I will call, following terminology suggested by Bruner and Kalmar (1998)[4], a *massive hermeneutical background* (MHB). But neither theory says much about it; they do not explain how we get this background, what sort of thing it is, or how precisely it comes into play when we attempt to use folk psychology or simulation.

On a nativist view of TT, which contends that a certain innate theory-of-mind module for social cognition simply comes online (around age 4 years) and allows us to reason our way into an understanding of others[5], solutions to the starting problem remain entirely mysterious. We simply have the capability and start using it when our brain is sufficiently developed. On a more empiricist view of TT one might argue that there is a natural connection between what I am calling the MHB and folk psychology (FP). On this view one might conceive of FP as a set of generalizations based on the MHB. We gain the MHB in lots and lots of observations of others, and from such experiences we simply abstract, through an inductive process, the general rules or theory of human behavior that constitutes FP. Gopnik and Meltzoff (1998)[6], for example, argue that young children are like scientists, constantly doing experiments (having experiences, playing, observing others) and generalizing across those experiments. FP, then, would be considered an abstract set of principles generated from the particularities of the MHB. Accordingly, I can simply draw on that background—the kind of very particular knowledge which comes from our experience of how people behave—to set the stage for the application of FP rules.

One might make a similar argument about simulation skills. On this view we could consider the MHB to consist in a learned set of skills or practical knowledge of how to deal with people. Thus, for either TT or ST, I know what rule or principle to apply, or what simulation to run, for any particular situation, because I draw on the particular knowledge or set of skills I have in the MHB.

Two conceptual problems follow from this way of thinking. First, if these empiricist accounts are accounts of how we acquire the MHB to support FP or, *mutatis mutandis*, simulation skills, they seem to presuppose that already within the MHB there is an implicit understanding of others. On the one hand, if there is not an intersubjective understanding already implicit in the MHB, then it is not clear how we could rely on it to specify a relevant FP rule or how it could be the basis for activating a simulation. That is, it is not clear how this would solve the starting problem. On the other hand, if there is an intersubjective understanding already implicit in the MHB, then it undermines the typical universal claim that normally goes along with TT or ST, namely, that FP or simulation, or some hybrid form of mindreading is the primary and pervasive way that we understand others.[7] Rather, this intersubjective understanding that is already implicit in the MHB would be developmentally primary. Moreover, if we rely on the MHB to get FP or simulation off the ground, then MHB would be as pervasive as FP or simulation. In that case, rather than primary and pervasive, FP or simulation may be secondary, and may be put into use only in situations where our interactions with others break down and the resources of the MHB are not sufficient to deliver a good understanding of others.

Second, if there is already an intersubjective understanding implicit in the MHB, it is not clear whether mindreading is simply a continuation of this kind of understanding, or constitutes something different, and if the latter, what that difference is. Is the application of FP a way of breaking away from this primary understanding, or a continuation of it? Are simulation skills of a different nature than the intersubjective skills implicit in the MHB, or if not, does that mean that the MHB is already a matter of simulation—simulation all the way down?

These issues motivate the following investigation into the nature of the MHB. The aim of this chapter is to take a close look at the MHB and to ask about its status in our everyday interactions with others. I will argue that the kind of understanding of others implicit in the MHB is not simply a precursor that is somehow replaced by FP or by a set of simulation skills[8], nor is it a form of theoretical inference or simulation, but is closely related to a set of ongoing embodied processes and narrative practices that characterize most of our everyday encounters with others. Much of what I have to say here, in the context of education, applies to very basic informal aspects of educational contexts, which nonetheless pervade any formal educational situation.

Background Conceptions

There are a number of conceptions of what we are calling "background" or the MHB. Searle , for example, considers the "Background" to be a set of capacities, abilities which constitute a general know-how and which allow us to function in everyday life.[9] For Searle, intentional phenomena "such as meanings, understandings, interpretations, beliefs, desires, and experiences only function within a set of Background capacities that are not themselves intentional".[10] The idea that the background capacities are themselves not intentional (understood in the Brentanian sense of intentionality) is motivated by the following thought. Any one intentional state (e.g., having a belief) is always part of a larger network of intentional states, but neither an intentional state on its own nor a set of intentional states is self-interpreting or self-applying. This is similar to what I am calling the starting problem or what in AI is called the "symbol grounding" problem. The question Searle is trying to answer is, what determines the conditions of satisfaction for any intentional state or any network of intentional states? His intuition is that the conditions of satisfaction for any intentional state are determined by a non-intentional set of capacities, for example, a set of sensory-motor capabilities. Searle offers an example from Wittgenstein. We look at a picture of a man walking uphill; but nothing in the picture itself specifies that the man is walking uphill rather than sliding back down the hill. What grounds our interpretation is our own experience of walking. If an intentional state is not cashed out in terms of some background capacity, skill, or practice, it would lead to an infinite regress in terms of trying to understand the meaning of the intentional state, much in the same way that in using a dictionary one can be led from the meaning of one word to the meaning of another, and from there to the meaning of another word, *ad infinitum.*

Searle's argument is based on linguistics and most of his examples come from language use. "Sally gave John the key, and he opened the door."[11]

This, like any sentence, is underdetermined with regard to its meaning. We understand the sentence to mean that Sally first gave John the key, and he then used it to open the door. But this understanding involves unstated content that we seemingly have to add to the sentence to make sense of it. This cannot be accomplished by adding more words to the sentence; that would simply introduce more underdetermined elements. Rather, the meaning is fixed by our practices and our know-how about how keys and doors work. Practices and know-how are not simply other sentences; they involve moving around the world and doing things.

There are some issues here that I will set aside for purposes of this chapter, but let me note that Searle changes his mind about the non-intentional status of the background;[12] the background includes both intentional and non-intentional states. For our purposes we shall set this issue aside and simply say that the background includes all kinds of capacities, practices, skills, and some finite range of knowing-how and knowing-that. Whether we want to say that all of these things are intentional (on a wide definition that would include things like motor intentionality) or not, should not matter for our purposes here.

Another issue concerns the question of whether we should think of the background as somehow reducible to brain processes. *Contra* Searle, I want to argue that the background, which includes cultural elements, is not reducible to neurophysiological capacity.[13] One way to see this is to think of how the background comes into our everyday practices. In this regard Bourdieu's notion of *habitus* is useful.[14] We can think of *habitus* as an individual's particular background. As such, *habitus* is a system of long-term, acquired dispositions (habits, schemas) of perception, thought, and action. These cognitive and somatic dispositions are not consciously manifest in our practices, but they function prenoetically, that is, they shape our experiences without our being aware that they are doing so. They are formed in response to physical and social environmental factors, and in this respect they are not reducible to neurophysiological states.

Consider some basic somatic aspects of *habitus*. Physical skills, for example, are not unrelated to posture and gait. The latter, however, are not simply a matter of a functioning basal ganglia and connected brain areas, but depend in essential ways on specifics of the body—flexibility of the joints, muscle tone, bone structure, etc.—as well as immediately present and long-term factors of the physical, social, and cultural environments.[15] These factors—brain, body, environment—are all part of one system. If I live in the mountains or teach at Cornell, my physical condition and way of moving may be very different than if I live in the desert or teach at NYU.

If I live immersed in a hip-hop culture, it is very likely that my gait is affected by a cultured movement; if I am a ballet dancer, or a military officer, my posture is likely quite different from that of the general population. More generally, what I am able to do and the particular skills I have are enabled and limited by the particular culture that I live in, which contributes to and in specific ways sets my *habitus*. It may be that the basal ganglia, and possibly other areas of the brain, of the ballet dancer are somewhat different from the same areas of the Cornell cosmologist, or the desert dweller. But it is not that difference that would constitute the full story of one's posture or gait or specific capabilities and skills. One's movement history is not inscribed like a text in the motor areas of the brain—no one can simply read it off of a perfect brain scan—although it is clear that one's movement history has literally (physically) shaped parts of the brain and have specified some of the details of how they function.

Likewise, one's life narrative is not inscribed like a text in one's brain, yet the details of one's life, in broad strokes, do have serious effects on various aspects of neural function. What precisely does the pre-frontal cortex look like in a person who was raised in an apartheid regime and told throughout his life that he is incapable of helping himself, and, as a result, has become convinced by this message and is unable to see any other possibilities? The complete structure of this way of being-in-the-world is not something that can be explained by neurophysiology.

The background, having its effects through an individual *habitus*, is a normative force that plays an essential role in regulating social practices, and contributing to social reproduction. Through deep educational processes, including formal educational practices which are themselves shaped by background conditions, individuals learn to act in ways that are appropriate to the possibilities provided for them. On Bourdieu's analysis, they learn to expect nothing different. Such dispositions tend to generate the same dispositions in others, and thus a certain normative order.

The background, considered not as narrowly neurobiological, but as widely embodied and embedded in practices that are not only physical but also social and cultural, is hermeneutical, in the sense that it shapes the way that individuals interpret their experience. The shaping process is both constraining and productive, reflecting hermeneutical principles well defined by the hermeneutical tradition.[16]

In the following sections I shall argue that the MHB, as it relates to an individual's capacity for intersubjective understanding, finds its beginning as an individual *habitus* in interactive intersubjective practices, and, through narrative practices, is further built up to include social and cultural norms.

First-Order Intersubjective Interactions

To bring the conception of the MHB to bear on the starting problem in social cognition, I want to point to two areas of research that are equally important for educational contexts. The first (discussed in this section) involves developmental evidence about how infants in the first 2 years of life interact with others. The second (in the next section) involves the development of narrative competency from the age of 2 years onward. I want to suggest (in the concluding section) that especially with regard to the questions raised in the first section about TT, ST, and the MHB, there is an alternative approach, based on both embodied processes of interaction and the acquisition of narrative competency, that provides a better account of our understanding of others and a better answer in regard to the role of the MHB in resolving the starting problem.

The beginning of this alternative account is to be found by looking at the first months of post-natal life. Although on the classical accounts of theory of mind, the child has to wait until the age of 4 years for important cognitive capacities for understanding others to kick in, on the alternative account the capacities for human interaction and intersubjective understanding are already accomplished in certain embodied processes that start early in infancy. These processes are emotional, sensory-motor, and perceptual. They include imitation (including neonate imitation), the parsing of perceived intentions[17], emotional interchange[18] and generally the processes that fall under the heading of primary intersubjectivity[19]. These are embodied practices that constitute our primary access for understanding others, and they continue to do so even after we attain our more sophisticated abilities in this regard.[20]

A primary, perceptual sense of others is already implicit in the behavior of the newborn infant. The newborn is able to imitate the facial gestures (e.g., tongue protrusion, mouth opening, pursing of the lips) presented by others.[21] In neonate imitation infants are able to distinguish between inanimate objects and human agents.[22] This depends not only on a contrast between self (minimally, a proprioceptive registration of one's own body) and non-self, but also on a responsiveness to the fact that the other is of the same sort as oneself, reflected in an intermodal relationship between the proprioception of one's own body and the perceived face of the other person.[23] Thus, for the infant, from the very start, the other person's body presents opportunities for imitative action and expressive behavior. There develops, from this initial kind of primary-intersubjective interaction, a common bodily intentionality that is shared by the perceiving subject and the perceived other, something which Merleau-Ponty called "intercorporeity."[24]

The early capabilities that contribute to primary intersubjectivity constitute a form of interaction that is not equivalent to mindreading, as construed in classical ToM accounts. Infants, notably without the intervention of theory or simulation, are able to see other people as agents, and to perceive bodily movement as goal-directed intentional movement. Infants at 10–11 months are able to parse some kinds of continuous action according to intentional boundaries.[25] Infants in the first year of life develop the ability to follow the other person's eyes, and to perceive various movements of the head, the mouth, the hands, and more general body movements as meaningful, goal-directed movements. Such perceptions provide nonconceptual, action-oriented understandings of the intentions and dispositions of other persons; they do not involve mindreading or inferences about beliefs or desires understood as mental states.[26]

Affective coordination between the gestures and expressions of the infant and those of caregivers with whom they interact is also an important part of primary intersubjectivity. Infants "vocalize and gesture in a way that seems 'tuned' [affectively and temporally] to the vocalizations and gestures of the other person."[27] Infants at 5–7 months detect correspondences between visual and auditory information that specify the expression of emotions.[28] Again, this does not involve taking a theoretical stance or creating a simulation of some inner mental state, but is a perceptual experience of an embodied comportment. In seeing the actions and expressive movements of the other person one is already perceiving their meaning; no inference to a hidden set of mental states (beliefs, desires, etc.) is necessary. In primary intersubjectivity, there is a common bodily intentionality that is shared across the perceiving subject and the perceived other. As Gopnik and Meltzoff indicate, "we innately map the visually perceived motions of others onto our own kinesthetic sensations."[29]

With these early capacities for human interaction, intersubjective perception and emotional resonance we begin to pick up implicitly the huge amount of social knowledge and intersubjective know-how that constitutes the MHB and shapes our *habitus*. It is important to keep in mind, however, that primary intersubjectivity is not primary simply in developmental terms. It does not characterize a stage that we go through and then leave behind. These capacities are not precursors to the "real thing"; they are the "real thing." They constitute important aspects of social cognition; they remain primary across all face-to-face intersubjective experiences, and they continue to characterize adult interactions. They contribute to the MHB not simply by providing factual information about others, but by constituting the ongoing implicit skills that we continue to use in our everyday dealings with others. They underpin those developmentally later, and rare, practices that may involve theorizing about or simulating mental states in others.

The face-to-face interactions that characterize primary intersubjectivity, however, do not exhaust the possibilities of intersubjective understanding. Expressions, intonations, gestures, and movements, along with the bodies that manifest them, do not float freely in thin air; we find them situated in the world. At around 1 year of age (possibly as early as 9 months), especially with the onset of joint attention, infants start to notice how others interact with the surrounding things in the physical environment. They begin to tie actions to pragmatic contexts, and acquire capacities of "secondary intersubjectivity."[30] They enter into *contexts* of shared attention—shared situations, shared interactions—in which they learn what things mean and what they are for. Behavior representative of joint attention begins to develop around 9–14 months.[31] Infants begin to see that another's movements and expressions are often mediated by the surrounding world. They see the other person's actions as meaningful and as framed in pragmatic contexts.

In joint attention the child alternates between monitoring the gaze of the other and what the other is gazing at, checking to verify that they are continuing to look at the same thing. The child also learns to point at approximately this same time. Eighteen-month-old children comprehend what another person intends to do with an instrument in a specific context. They are able to re-enact to completion the goal-directed behavior that someone else fails to complete. Thus, the child, on seeing an adult who tries to manipulate a toy and who appears frustrated about being unable to do so, quite readily picks up the toy and shows the adult how to do it.[32]

In understanding the actions of others we understand actions at the most relevant pragmatic (intentional, goal-oriented) level. In our everyday interactions we clearly ignore possible sub-personal or lower-level descriptions. But, for the most part, we also ignore interpretations in terms of beliefs, desires, or hidden mental states. Rather than making mindreading inferences to what the other person intends by starting with visible behaviors, and moving thence to the level of mental events, we see actions as meaningful in the contexts of the physical and intersubjective environment. We interpret the actions of others in terms of their goals and intentions set in pragmatically or socially contextualized situations, rather than abstractly in terms of either their muscular performance or their mental states. Accordingly, the situation is never perceived neutrally (without meaning), either in regard to our own possible actions, or in regard to the actions and possibilities of others. As Heidegger's analysis of *Zuhandenheit*,[33] and Gibson's theory of affordances suggest,[34] we see things enactively, primarily in relation to their possible uses, and as such we are not passive observers. Likewise, our perception of the other person, as another agent, is never of an entity existing outside of a situation; rather we perceive the other enactively, as an agent with whom we can interact.

The capabilities for understanding others that define primary and secondary intersubjectivity—the embodied, sensory-motor (emotion informed) capabilities that enable us to perceive the intentions of others (from birth onward), and the perceptual and action capabilities that enable us to understand others in the pragmatically contextualized situations of everyday life (from 9–18 months onward)—are not themselves sufficient to address what are clearly new developments that come online around the ages of 2, 3, and 4 years. Quite obviously, language starts to play an important role around the age of 2 years. But language development itself is something that depends on some of the capabilities of primary and secondary intersubjectivity. In turn, language carries these capabilities forward and puts them into service in much more sophisticated social contexts that involve communicative and narrative competencies.

Narrative Competence

How do we get the more complex and nuanced understandings of why people do what they do? Together we live in the frameworks of important institutions—educational, legal, cultural—and we engage in complex social practices. To understand others in these situations and to engage in such practices we need something more than our basic perceptions, emotions, and embodied interactions, even those that are defined in pragmatic and basic social contexts. Is this where we need to turn to folk psychology or simulation? I shall suggest in this section that we extend our developed abilities for understanding others through communicative and narrative practices rather than through the employment of theory or simulation. My focus will be on narrative. The pervasive presence of narrative in our daily lives, and the development of narrative competency, can provide not only a more parsimonious alternative to theory or simulation approaches, and a better way to account for the more nuanced understandings (and misunderstandings) we have of others, but also an account of how the MHB gets built up.

Again, we can learn a great deal from developmental psychology. As we saw, around the age of two, children possess capacities for embodied and contextualized understandings. Young children are practiced in understanding things as other people understand them in pragmatic contexts, and when the capacities associated with primary and secondary intersubjectivity are combined with several other newly acquired capacities (including language use and episodic memory), young children are ready to understand things and people in emerging narrative structures. Narratives, made available to the child by caregivers, for example, or generated in interactive contexts by others, and eventually by the child, are, in the first place, stories about actions and interactions. They often include reasons for acting. That is, they tell us about people in specific situations, what they do, how they interact with others, and they sometimes indicate the motives that people have for doing what they do. Each *persona dramatis* is represented with their own dispositions and traits, and is situated in particular surroundings that evoke certain emotions. The way a person's story unfolds will depend on his or her unique history, overarching projects and interactions among other characters involved. Through such narratives we gain interpretive insights into the actions of others. As a result, these insights are added to the growing body of background knowledge (the MHB) that we have about others.

Narratives, however, give us more than their contents. They give us a form or structure that we can use in understanding others. That is, we learn from narrative how to frame an understanding of others. We start to see others, engaged in their actions, not simply in terms of the immediate and occurrent context. We start to see them as engaged in longer-term projects (plots) that add meaning to what they are doing. Just as an isolated gesture (a gesture that has no context) has little meaning, but gains in meaning as we see it in context—a waving hand on its own might mean a variety of things, but will take on a specific meaning when a police officer is waving at me as I drive toward her—so also a specific context for which we have no narrative framework may have less meaning than a context that fits into an extended and storied pattern of activity.

This does not mean that our understanding of others requires an occurrent or explicit narrative story telling, but it does require the ability to see or to frame the other person in a detailed pragmatic or social context, and to understand that context in a narrative way. As Alasdair MacIntyre suggested, for an observer, or for a participant, an action has intelligibility when it can find a place in a narrative.[35]

Young children exposed to narratives (about others, about imaginary characters, about themselves, etc.) learn to "frame" other persons (as well as themselves) and the relevant contexts in narrative. When children listen to stories, or see them enacted (in various media), or when they themselves play-act (and the same applies to adults who are exposed to parables, plays, myths, novels, films, television, etc.) they become familiarized with sets of characters and with a range of ordinary or extraordinary situations, and the sorts of actions appropriate to those situations.[36] All of this helps to shape their expectations. An education in narratives of many sorts provides knowledge of what actions are acceptable and in what circumstances, what sort of events are important and noteworthy, what accounts can account for action, and what kind of explanations constitute the giving of good reasons. In other words, narratives instil norms and shape our understanding of what we and others are doing.

Children are clearly supported in this process by caregivers and teachers. They are often provided with running commentaries on stories that teach them not only which actions are appropriate in particular situations but also what reasons for acting are and are not acceptable. Narratives provide the standards by which we judge an action's appropriateness. Even if, as often happens, in time such standards are challenged and overturned, that critical process is almost always accomplished within the medium of further narratives. Stories—even in their particularities, whether real or fictional—teach us what others can expect from us, but just as importantly, what we can expect from others in certain situations. Through narratives we not only come to know what others ought to (and thus are likely to) do, but also what they ought to (and thus are likely to) think and feel, and this is indexed to the particular kind of person they are. Through the pervasive narratives of our childhood and through the continuing narratives of adult life we learn the *norms* associated with social roles encountered in our everyday environments—in the shops, restaurants, homes, theaters, and various social and cultural institutions in which we live and do what we do.

That narratives engage our interpretive abilities means something more than simply the exercise of a cognitive ability, or a passive appropriation of content. Our engagement with narratives presupposes a wide range of emotive and interactive abilities. To appreciate such stories children must be capable of the sort of emotional response found in basic social engagements.[37] The kind of emotional resonance that one finds in primary intersubjectivity, for example, plays an important role in narrative practice. Evidence for this can be found in a recent fMRI study.[38] Subjects were presented with a series of video clips showing actors telling sad and neutral stories, as if they had personally experienced them. The stories were told with either congruent or incongruent facial expressions of emotion.

Subjects were then asked to rate the mood of the actor and how likable they found that person. Watching sad stories versus neutral stories was associated with increased processing activity in emotion related structures (including the amygdala and parieto-frontal areas, predominantly in the right hemisphere). These areas were not activated when the narrator showed incongruent facial expressions, however. Conflict between what we sense as the emotional state of the person, simply on the basis of seeing his face and expressive actions, and the narrative content he presents, is disruptive to understanding. Whatever is going on in the brain correlates not simply to features of action and expression (and the subjectivity) of the person we are trying to understand (the narrator in this case), but to the larger story, the scene, the circumstance recounted in the narrative, and how features of the person's action and expression match or fail to match those circumstances.

In gaining an understanding of another person, then, it is not always (and perhaps not frequently) a matter of characterizing the other's mental life, understood as a kind of hidden inner life, but simply the other's life as it unfolds in response to worldly/situational contexts. Such things are best captured in a narrative form. Coming to understand another's reasons should not be understood as inferring or simulating their discrete "mental states," but as grasping their action-oriented attitudes and responses as whole situated persons. I encounter the other person, not abstracted from their circumstances, but in the middle of something that has a beginning and that is going somewhere. I see them in the framework of a story in which either I have a part to play or I do not. The narrative is not primarily about what is going on "inside their heads"; it is about what is going on in their world, or in the world that we share, and the way they understand and respond to it.

Narrative practices feed and are fed by the MHB. An understanding informed by the MHB does not take the form of grasping a set of explicit FP generalizations about how others will act. Rather, one learns a set of cultural norms and expectations through interactive and narrative practices such that these become second nature, a *habitus*. Furthermore, by learning how certain characters in our bedtime stories behave or ought to behave, and by learning how I ought to behave in such and such a circumstance, I learn how you ought to behave as well. This provides me with certain guiding expectations about your behaviour (a certain set of possibilities) in so far as you do not behave abnormally, and, by definition, that is the case for most people most of the time. Learning such norms through narrative practice does not take the form of internalizing an explicit set of rules (or a set of theoretical propositions). It involves becoming accustomed to particular norms, coming to embody them, or being able to enact them, as it were, through practice and habit.

Conclusion

On one account competency with different kinds of narratives enables us to understand others in a variety of ways, specifically by allowing us to develop a folk psychology.[39] This is what Hutto calls the narrative practice hypothesis: "The core claim of the Narrative Practice Hypothesis (or NPH) is that direct encounters with stories about reasons for acting, supplied in interactive contexts by responsive caregivers, is the normal route through which children become familiar with both (i) the core structure of folk psychology and (ii) the norm-governed possibilities for wielding it in practice, knowing *how* and knowing *when* to use it."[40] I suggest that we can put this in terms of the MHB rather than in terms of FP. That is, I think that narratives, which are made available to children by their caregivers and are also generated in interactive contexts, and which are, in the first place, about actions and interactions, contribute to the MHB from which our more sophisticated understandings of others continue to draw sustenance. We can then think of FP as an abstracted version of the MHB, put to use in certain rare situations as one way to understand another's reasons for acting. In line with Hutto, this means that we should talk about FP practice rather than FP as a theory.[41]

In addition, this view of narrative practice addresses the starting problem. We learn through narratives *how* and *when* to use FP, and we draw on primary and secondary intersubjective skills implicit in the MHB to get the process off the ground. The use of FP—that is, the practice of drawing folk-psychological platitudes from the MHB to explain the actions of others—is, however, relatively rare in our everyday interactions. Primary and secondary intersubjective processes, as well as narrative competencies for understanding others, provide most of what we need for understanding others. In those cases where we may be puzzled by another's actions, or in cases where we are confined to an observational stance, without good access to the context of someone's actions, or where we may have to give an explanatory account of someone's actions, then we may indeed appeal to FP, or to a special set of simulation skills drawn from the wealth of know-how provided by the MHB.

Even if in the unusual case, where we are observers of an unfamiliar action in a strange setting carried out by someone we do not know, and we turn to an explicit use of FP, we never do this outside of a narrative framework. Rather, we attempt to see an action as in some way coherent and meaningful by testing out plot structures, by framing it in a story that would make sense of it. If we are asked to explain it, it is likely that we will explain it narratively, in terms of what the person is doing in what seems to be the situation. There is no other way to get to the more abstract level of discourse in which we attribute beliefs and desires to the person.

In other words, if or when it comes to mindreading—employing FP or a set of simulation skills—such practices get off the ground only because interactive (primary and secondary intersubjective) capabilities provide a starting point, and narrative competency provides a framework for intersubjective understanding. Both interactive and narrative processes contribute to the formation of the MHB, and the MHB in turn informs narrative and interactive processes.

I have argued in this chapter that interactive processes, which allow us to perceive the feelings and intentions of others in their movements, gestures, facial expressions, and actions, feed into the development of more nuanced intersubjective understandings found in narrative practices. Narratives are complex objects of joint attention, and they can function as such in educational contexts. They emerge out of first-order interactions and reflect those interactions in their content. In most everyday cases, interactive and narrative practices provide all we need for understanding others. Only rarely do we need to appeal to standard theory-of-mind (TT or ST) explanations. In those rare cases, theoretical or simulationist practices get off the ground or find their starting point in the MHB, which finds its beginning as an individual *habitus* in interactive intersubjective practices, and, through narrative practices, is further built up to include social and cultural norms.

Notes

1 The author thanks the University of Central Florida for sabbatical support in Fall 2009, and acknowledges support for this research from multiple grants: a CNRS Research Grant as Visiting Scholar at the Centre de Recherche en Epistémelogie Appliquée (CREA), Paris; National Science Foundation grant (# 0639037), and the European Science Foundation project *Consciousness in a Natural and Cultural Context* (BASIC).

2 See Gallagher, "Logical and Phenomenological Arguments Against Simulation Theory," in D. Hutto and M. Ratcliffe, eds., *Folk Psychology Re-assessed* (New York: Springer Publishers, 2007a), 63–78; and Gallagher, "Simulation Trouble," *Social Neuroscience* 2 (3–4) (2007b), 353–65.

3 (Goldman, "Imitation, Mind Reading, and Simulation," in S. Hurley and N. Chater, eds., *Perspectives on Imitation II* (Cambridge, MA: MIT Press, 2005), 80–1.

4 Bruner and Kalmar, "Narrative and Metanarrative in the Construction of Self," in M. Ferrari and R. J. Sternberg, eds., *Self-Awareness: Its Nature and Development* (New York: Guilford Press, 1998), 308–31.

[5] For example, Carruthers, "Simulation and Self-Knowledge: A Defence of the Theory-Theory," in P. Carruthers and P. K. Smith, eds. *Theories of Theories of Mind* (Cambridge: Cambridge University Press, 1996); and Scholl and Leslie, "Modularity, Development and Theory of Mind," *Mind and Language* 14 (1) (1999) 131–53.

[6] Gopnik and Meltzoff, *Words, Thoughts, and Theories* (Cambridge, MA: MIT Press, 1998).

[7] The frequently made claim is that in all cases when we encounter others we attempt to explain or predict their behavior by inferring or simulating mental states, or that such theoretical or simulation stances are the default. See, for example, Baron-Cohen, *Mindblindness: An Essay on Autism and Theory of Mind* (Cambridge, MA: MIT Press, 1995), 3–4); Goldman "Simulation Theory and Mental Concepts," in J. Dokic and J. Proust, eds., *Simulation and Knowledge of Action* (Amsterdam/Philadephia: John Benjamins, 2002), 7–8.

[8] See, for example, Baron-Cohen, *Mindblindness*; Currie, "Some Ways of Understanding People," *Philosophical Explorations* 11 (3) (2008), 211–18; Gallagher, "Inference or Interaction: Social Cognition Without Precursors," *Philosophical Explorations* 11 (3) (2008), 163–73.

[9] Searle, "Literal Meaning," *Erkenntnis* 1 (1978), 207–24; Searle, *The Rediscovery of the Mind* (Cambridge, MA: MIT Press, 1992).

[10] Searle, *The Rediscovery of the Mind*, 175.

[11] Ibid., 181.

[12] Ibid., 186ff.

[13] Searle is an internalist who thinks that all factors that contribute to cognition must be cashed out in neurophysiological terms; he writes: "The occurrent ontology of those parts of the Network that are unconscious is that of a neurophysiological capacity, but the Background consists entirely in such capacities." See Searle, *The Rediscovery of the Mind*, 188.

[14] Bourdieu, "Structures, Habitus, Practices," in P. Bourdieu, *The Logic of Practice* (Stanford, CA: Stanford University Press, 1990), 52–79.

[15] Gallagher, *How the Body Shapes the Mind* (Oxford: Oxford University Press, 2005).

[16] See Gadamer, *Truth and Method*, trans. J. Weinsheimer and D. G.Marshall, 2nd rev. edition (New York: Crossroad, 1989); Gallagher, *Hermeneutics and Education*. (Albany: State University of New York Press, 1992).

[17] Baldwin , D. A., Baird, J. A., Saylor, M. M. and Clark, M. A. "Infants Parse Dynamic Action." *Child Development* 72 (3) (2001), 708–17.

[18] Hobson, *The Cradle of Thought: Exploring the Origins of Thinking* (Oxford: Oxford University Press, 2004).

[19] Trevarthen, "Communication and Cooperation in Early Infancy: A Description of Primary Intersubjectivity." in M. Bullowa, ed., *Before Speech* (Cambridge: Cambridge University Press), 1979.

[20] Gallagher, *How the Body Shapes the Mind*.

[21] Meltzoff and Moore, "Imitation of Facial and Manual Gestures by Human Neonates," *Science* 7 (4312) (1977), 75–8.

[22] Johnson, "The Recognition of Mentalistic Agents in Infancy," *Trends in Cognitive Science* 4 (2000), 22–8; Legerstee "The Role of Person and Object in Eliciting Early Imitation," *Journal of Experimental Child Psychology* 51 (1991), 423–33.

[23] Gallagher and Meltzoff, "The Earliest Sense of Self and Others: Merleau-Ponty and Recent Developmental Studies." *Philosophical Psychology* 9 (1996), 213–36.

[24] Merleau-Ponty, *The Visible and the Invisible*, trans. A. Lingis (Evanston: Northewestern University Press, 1969).

[25] Baldwin et al., "Infants Parse Dynamic Action," 708–17.

[26] Allison, Puce, and McCarthy, "Social Perception from Visual Cues: Role of the STS Region," *Trends in Cognitive Science* 4 (7) (2000), 267–78; Baldwin, "Infants' Ability to Consult the Speaker for Clues to Word Reference," *Journal of Child Language* 20 (1993), 395–418; Gallagher, "The Practice of Mind: Theory, Simulation or Primary Interaction?" *Journal of Consciousness Studies* 8 (5–7) (2001), 83–108; Johnson, "The Recognition of Mentalistic Agents in Infancy," 22–8.

[27] Gopnik and Meltzoff, *Words, Thoughts, and Theories*, 131.

[28] Walker, "Intermodal Perception of Expressive Behaviors by Human Infants," *Journal of Experimental Child Psychology* 33 (1982), 514–35.

[29] Gopnik and Meltzoff, *Words, Thoughts, and Theories*, 129. This idea is fully consistent with both recent neuroscientific evidence about mirror neurons and Husserl's views on the phenomenology of kinaesthesis (see Gallagher, *How the Body Shapes the Mind*).

[30] Trevarthen and Hubley, "Secondary Intersubjectivity: Confidence, Confiding and Acts of Meaning in the First Year," in A. Lock, ed., *Action, Gesture and Symbol: The Emergence of Language* (London: Academic Press, 1978), 183–229.

[31] Phillips, Baron-Cohen, and Rutter, "The Role of Eye Contact in the Detection of Goals: Evidence from Normal Toddlers, and Children with Autism or Mental Handicap," *Development and Psychopathology* 4 (1992), 375–83; Reddy, *How Infants Know Minds*. (Cambridge, MA: Harvard University Press), 2008.

[32] Meltzoff, "Understanding the Intentions of Others: Re-enactment of Intended Acts by 18-Month-Old Children," *Developmental Psychology* 31 (1995), 838–50.

[33] Heidegger, *Being and Time*, trans. J. Macquarrie and E. Robinson (London: SCM Press, 1962).

[34] Gibson, *The Ecological Approach to Visual Perception* (Boston: Houghton Mifflin, 1979).

[35] Alasdair MacIntyre, *After Virtue* (South Bend: University of Notre Dame Press, 1981).

[36] "Children's first narrative productions occur in action, in episodes of symbolic play by groups of peers, accompanied by—rather than solely through—language. Play is an important developmental source of narrative" (Nelson "Narrative and the Emergence of a Consciousness of Self," in G. D. Fireman, T. E. J. McVay and O. Flanagan, eds., *Narrative and Consciousness* (Oxford: Oxford University Press, 2003), 28; also see Richner and Nicolopoulou, "The Narrative Construction of Differing Conceptions of the Person in the Development of Young Children's Social Understanding," in *Early Education and Development* 12 (2001), 393–432).

[37] Gallagher, "The Narrative Alternative to Theory of Mind," *Consciousness and Emotion: Special Issue on Radical Enactivism* 7 (2006).

[38] Decety and Chaminade, "Neural Correlates of Feeling Sympathy," *Neuropsychologia* 41 (2003), 127–8.

[39] Hutto, *Folk Psychological Narratives: The Socio-Cultural Basis of Understanding Reasons* (Cambridge, MA: MIT Press, 2008).

[40] Hutto, "The Narrative Practice Hypothesis," in D. D. Hutto, ed., *Narrative and Understanding Persons*, Royal Institute of Philosophy Supplement (Cambridge: Cambridge University Press, 2007); see Gallagher and Hutto, "Understanding Others Through Primary Interaction and Narrative Practice," in J. Zlatev, T. Racine, C. Sinha and E. Itkonen, eds., *The Shared Mind: Perspectives on Intersubjectivity* (Amsterdam: John Benjamins, 2008), 17–38.

[41] Hutto, *Folk Psychological Narratives*.

Chapter 3

Philosophical Hermeneutics: An Education for all Seasons?

Nicholas Davey

Philosophy has an obligation to take into account all experience that is part of the human condition.

—*John Cottingham.*[1]

Prelude: Three Concepts

This chapter is built upon mutually interwoven concepts. The following definitions are not definitive but offer descriptions which set the context of our argument. 1. Education: to bring up, provide schooling or tuition, from the Latin, *educare*, related and *educere* to lead or draw forth, to bring out or develop from a latent condition.[2] 2. *Bildung:* a complex German term relating to the process of education, cultural development and the processes of individual and social formation. Wilhelm Humboldt (1767–1835) brings the concept to a point of high development in German thought. Although it is associated with the Romantic ideal of achieving "a harmonious individuality nourished by the diversity of experience," *Bildung* equally evokes notions of an inner, spontaneous vitality and "of an underlying coherence or pattern working itself out through an immense diversity and gaining nourishment from it, and of a creative reciprocal relation to experience, in which even error and suffering are made meaningful through the concept of education."[3] 3. Philosophical hermeneutics: Hans-Georg Gadamer's term for the attempt to navigate philosophically what happens to us when we are addressed by the event of a profound experience or of a text "speaking to us." What governs the possibility of experience's formative power?[4]

Speaking of Humboldt, John Burrows notes that "*Bildung* could be represented as a quasi-organic and dialectical process, consisting of endless acceptances and innumerable provisional reconciliations of the creative tension between the individual and his [or her] environment and between the various contending aspects of his own nature."[5] However, as we shall see, it is important to distinguish between (1) *Bildung* as a formative process and (2) the idealized ends of *Bildung*, its alleged goals. Ernst Cassirer's argument that no author can imagine the multiple determinations his or her concept will acquire in its subsequent history rings true of the *Begriffsgeschichte* attached to *Bildung*.[6] Though its provenance lies deep in the German linguistic imagination rather than in the mind of a single author, the quite different endeavors of Goethe's aesthetics of self-formation and Nietzsche's warring individualism attest to the various, even contradictory, determinations the concept of *Bildung* sustains. Many of the ends arguments (especially those which elevate a bourgeois ideal of "cultured" education) have brought the term *Bildung* into disrepute, but this mistakes the means for the end of the process. The continuing educational relevance of *Bildung* lies in the formative and not the ends arguments. The proper end of the *Bildung* process is the continual intensification of individual and social capacities for self-transformation: the pursuit of a (historically mutable) ideal end is merely a galvanizing means of achieving the proper end of continuous transformation, not the end of transformation itself. Indeed, the anthropological dimensions of *Bildung* as a formative process suggest that positing any end-state for its development is a contradiction in terms. This chapter will argue that a repertoire of intellectual manoeuvres within philosophical hermeneutics demonstrate the continuing powerful relevance of *Bildung* to current social, cultural, and educational debate.

A Late Guest

Given the skepticism many postmodern thinkers have towards the ideals of Europe's long tradition of education, the emergence of Gianni Vattimo as a defender of *Bildung* speaks well of the continuing legacy and legitimacy of the concept. Vattimo's dialogical utopianism makes an apt contribution to current social debate in that it seeks not the restoration of an economic equilibrium *without* unemployment but the defense of every individual's entitlement to a meaningful existence. This is not understood as the realization of some metaphysical end-state but as the intensification of qualitative aspects of existence: "*Solidarity* rather than competition *is implied*," "the reduction of all forms of violence rather than the affirmation of metaphysical principles or the endorsement of scientific models of society."[7] Progress is not the fulfillment of an anticipated end but the process which makes further development possible. Heidegger's ontology and the German romantic concept of *Bildung* shape Vattimo's political vision. A personal commitment to difference and diversity is supported by his adherence to Heidegger's conception of the unfolding of Being as "event." Accordingly, Vattimo argues that individuals have the right to "freely project themselves" in a reasonably justified manner by shaping and giving meaning to their life-world without violently encroaching on other persons. "Culture," he argues, "no longer stems from the assumption of heredity but from an ever new self-description culminating in an existential self-creation that replaces the ideal of handed-down knowledge."[8] Furthermore, "the ultimate goal of philosophical investigation after the end of metaphysics is no longer contact with something existing independently from us, but rather *Bildung*, the unending formation of oneself."[9]

This social and political perspective has distinct theological undertones. The outcome of unending individual qualitative transformation is not conceived as eventually arriving in a promised land but as a graceful acceptance of what humans are: creatures whose essence resides in tireless negotiation and transformation. Such anthropological non-essentialism favors hermeneutics as a mode of cultural rationale. "Weak thought" does not ascribe any rigid content to the idea of what is and what is not human. Vattimo's disputes with government and church over sexual prejudice concern over-restrictive assumptions about what is and is not human. If human beings have no predetermined essence, what they are is the consequence of continuous adaption and negotiation. As Michael Oakeshott will argue, what they may yet become depends on continuous exchange with others, challenging and extending horizons of individual and collective possibility.

These theological and anthropological underpinnings push Vattimo into a position of controversy. They imply a rejection of any constitutional fixity as permanent since legal and political definition involves a degree of forceful imposition. On the other hand, the anti-constitutionalist's dependence upon debate and precedence is completely consistent with Vattimo's hermeneutical orientation. The role of *Bildung* in Vattimo's social and political thought is far from anachronistic and demonstrates the vital relevance of the term in contemporary debates about education and social philosophy.

The key points we can take from Vattimo are: 1. *The right of all individuals to quest for a meaningful existence.* From the point of view of the present argument, it is not the question of right which is important but the equating of individual existence and a quest for meaningfulness. 2. *Progress understood not as the achievement of an end-state but the intensification of formative processes which are sharpened by the pursuit of such an end.* This, as we shall see, nudges the notion of *Bildung* towards a practiced disposition towards openness. 3. *The recognition that cultural and educative principles are without foundation and best understood as articulating processes of unending formation.* A hermeneutical philosophy such as Vattimo's is non-essentialist: cultural dialogue and transmission establish norms of wisdom and understanding which are then subject to interrogation by the very practices that establish them. *Bildung* concerns the possibility of collective as well as individual transformation. 4. *Open dialogue is a collective means of drawing out this potential.* The question here is whether dialogue can establish the conditions whereby a pre-established potential can be serendipitously drawn out or creates the possibility of unanticipated and new developments. These axioms derive from the three concepts outlined above and identify the underlying *Leitmotiven* of our argument.

Problem and Claim

Can there be a philosophy of education which overreaches the transient? The answer could be affirmative were it based on a credible essentialism which proclaimed the defining characteristics of human beings as being immune to change. With its commitment to historical mutability, such a proclamation would be a contradiction in terms for philosophical hermeneutics. The one principle of Enlightenment thought that philosophical hermeneutics wholeheartedly embraces is that of historical change. How, then, does philosophical hermeneutics establish a view of education which is neither essentialist nor merely an opportunist acquiescence to ever-changing political agendas? We shall argue that philosophical hermeneutics is able to found a philosophy of education which overreaches the transient precisely because of its emphasis on the educative process—*Bildung*—rather than upon the selection of an educational form. To demonstrate this will require an elaboration of the philosophical entailments within the *Leitmotifen* underpinning Vattimo's defense of *Bildung*.

Disappointed?

Change, whether in the shape of natural disaster, historical upheaval or technological transformation, invariably presents humanity with a challenge. Whether change is perceived as a threat or an opportunity depends upon complex expectations relating to notions of order and time. Harry Frankfurt cites ancient Egyptian texts from the time of the pyramid builders which react in horror to the disturbance of the established social order. "Neferrohu said: *I show thee the land in lamentation. The man with a weak arm (now) has (a strong) arm . . . I show thee how the undermost is turned uppermost. . . . The poor man will acquire riches.*" The most famous of the sages, Ipuwer, is even more explicit. For instance, he condemns as a disastrous parody of order the fact that "*gold and lapis are hung about the necks of slave girls. But noble ladies walk through the land and mistresses of houses say: 'Would that we had something to eat. . . . Behold they that possessed beds now lie upon the ground. He that slept with dirt now stuffeth for himself a cushion.*'" The upshot is unmitigated misery for all.[10]

Nietzsche's analysis of the "egyptianism" within the Platonic tradition of European thought is instructive: a psychology (collective or individual) that holds Being and Eternity in high value will receive the fact of Becoming as an affront: "The world as it is ought not to be."[11] Heracleitus's *logos* (the measure that is in all change) and Nietzsche's *Ewige Wiederkehr* do not so much "egyptianize" change as allow a wise distance from it: we understand that change expresses a principled order in all phenomena, including ourselves. However, understanding that change is inevitable and unavoidable does not lessen the pain of bereavement or the departure of a loved one. Gadamer speaks accurately when he writes, "Experience is primarily an experience of negation: it [experience's object] is not, however, as we thought. In view of the experience that we have of another object, both things change, our knowledge and its object."[12] "Every experience worthy of the name runs counter to our expectation. Thus the historical nature of man contains as an essential element a fundamental negativity that emerges in the relation between experience and insight."[13] Philosophical hermeneutics does not ally itself explicitly with a philosophical anthropology and yet, if it did, the "negativity of experience" thesis and its related conception of education would be central to its articulation of such an anthropology.

Nothing is Standard

Philosophical hermeneutics is anti-essentialist. Following Nietzsche and Heidegger, it regards humanity as a life-group whose essence is essentially to be in question always. For such a life-group, survival is possible only on the basis of experiences which promote its well-being. However, within a continuously changing environment there is no guarantee that what has served group interests will continue to do so. When Gadamer speaks of *Dasein* which denotes human existence he specifically equates it with being-in-motion.[14] This neither implies *Werden* (becoming) conceived as a purposeful unfolding (Hegel) nor as a nihilistic flux (Nietzsche). It implies a process (being-in-the-world) which can only maintain its *being* by being-in-motion. Such a being must continually set itself at a distance from, review and move on from its present condition or formation. It is appropriate for such a life-group to continually provoke and challenge the viability of its accumulated experience. Gadamer perceives the core issue: "The nature of experience is conceived in terms of that which goes beyond it; for experience itself can never be a science. It is in absolute antithesis to knowledge and to that kind of instruction that follows from general and theoretical knowledge. The truth of experience always contains an orientation to new experience. . . . *The dialectic of experience has its own fulfilment not in definitive knowledge, but in that openness to experience that is encouraged by experience itself.*"[15]

Any parody of this as the "disappointment is character building" argument is rendered superficial by exposing the underlying concept cluster: the *experimentalism* that puts *experience* to the test (experiment and experience share the latin root *experiri*—to try) is *formative* (*Bildung*) of a way of life (*bios*) whose way is to question itself continually, to try, to test and trial its experience. The "subject" in question *is* indeed the subject-in-question.

Franciso Varela conceives of living systems as autopoietic insofar as they have no essence they appeal to in order to function.[16] An essence would not only lie outside and be structurally different from the inner workings of the living system but, being of a necessarily determinate character, it would limit disadvantageously the response capacity of that system to others. Varela observes, "As the system has no essence, it must avail itself of these previous behavioural patterns and process potentially all the efforts it has made to ensure self-maintenance, thus giving rise to its internal 'recursive history' . . . It has no goal outside itself and so it must take up what it has already developed earlier as guidance for maintaining self-organisation."[17] The world in which living systems find themselves is not inert but a living complexity of different autopoietic systems. Living systems do not perceive each other as actual objects but rather as a set of possibilities that actuality presents them with. According to John Shotter, living systems are always placed within a wider network of others: a system will always seek to orient itself to ever-changing circumstances which it perceives as possibilities for enhancement or for avoidance.[18] Varela, like Mikhail Bakhtin, sees living systems as developmental. Hence, both present communicative interactions as dialogical, as conversations which proceed recursively through a continual feed backward and forward throughout the different all levels of the system.[19] "Conversation has been a . . . paradigm for interactions among autonomous systems, and these two sides of it go together. Its role as the exemplary case of autonomous interaction comes from the fact that a conversation is direct experience, human experience par excellence—we live and breathe in dialogue and language, And from this direct experience we know that one cannot find a firm reference point for the content of dialogue."[20]

The most elemental fact, as Nietzsche calls it, is the *pathos* of every living system: its vulnerability, its susceptibility to other living systems from which its own becoming and effecting emerge.[21] A hermeneutical ontology is fundamental to Varela's and Iser's interactions theory. Indeed, it would not be inconsistent within this conceptual framework to see in the term "education"—to be drawn out, to be led out—something of the *pathos* of living beings, that is, living is equated with being drawn out by experience and dialogical exchange.

The summary points of these reflections are as follows. 1. The non-essentialist anthropology of thinkers such as Varela fits well with the ontological basis of Gadamer's philosophical hermeneutics. 2. Communicative *interaction* generates the processes which are both at the heart of and sustain each position. 3. Both Varela's non-essentialist anthropology and Gadamer's philosophical hermeneutics are sustained by mutually penetrating conceptual entailments attached to the terms experience, experiment, and education (formation). This triad is hermeneutically nuanced in that these terms are connected to communicative (interpretive) interaction, a nuance which is evident in Vattimo's appeal to *Bildung* collective exchange. 4. This conceptual triad entails the notion of hermeneutical processes which exhibit themselves only "in the doing." Motion and, hence, transformation (*Bildung*) an association of terms explicit in Gadamer's reasoning, will be central to the following argument.

Having established the ontological basis of our case, let us turn to the specifics of Gadamer's account of *Bildung*. Before we do, however, the context for making an important point is established. Philosophical hermeneutics does not defend or propose a particular view of education. It does not offer a specific educational programme. Neither does it propose one way of doing hermeneutics. What concerns philosophical hermeneutics above all are the transformative effects of an educational disposition which engages dialogically with the achievements of the cultural past and is open to responding to the unavoidable challenges of the future.

"Offne dich, mein ganzes Herze": Humanist (Re-)Formation

Gadamer's presentation of *Bildung* synthesizes Herder's understanding of the term with Hegel's and offers the following theses.[22]

1 *Bildung* as a process of self-formation is ontologically congruent with non-essentialism: "Man is characterised by the break with the immediate and the natural that the intellectual, rational side of his nature demands of him. . . . In this sphere he is not, by nature, what he should be, and hence he needs *Bildung*".[23] Corollary 1: human development does not take place *ex nihilo*. Neither does non-essentialism suppose that humanity is free to become anything it wishes. Though metaphysically contingent, human existence is dependent upon the received orientation of tradition. These, in effect, serve as constraints upon the direction of self-formation, limiting it but not controlling it while they also operate as a condition of experience itself.

2 *Bildung* is associated with the idea of culture insofar as it involves a contextualized development of inherent rather than innate natural talent and capacity.[24] Corollary 2: human capacities are a response to, are drawn out by and indeed reflect a cultural environment. Capacities are interactive rather than innate. They are processes which develop according to cultural location rather than unfolding according to an internal *logos*.

3 *Bildung* as effect. *Bildung*'s curricula may traditionally focus on classical languages or those of Asia and the Orient, but its focus is not necessarily on what it aims at. It actually aims at the acquisition of a certain mature poise with regard to the challenges of the unusual and unexpected. *Bildung* as formation describes the effect of an educative process rather than the means, that is, the aim is but a galvanizing device. *Bildung* is not achieved by means of technical instruction but grows out of engagement with a set of concerns. *Bildung* aspires to remain in a constant state of development. *Bildung* has no goal outside itself. Nor can it be a goal itself since it is an effect. It cannot be sought except in the reflective thematic of the educator. [25] Corollary 3: *Bildung* is not an end-state, but more a condition of acquired maturity which exhibits itself in both a receptive and reflective disposition to the lifelong challenge of experience. *Bildung* is a mature reflective sensibility formed from an engagement with the world and its concerns and maintained in the continuing movement that openness to experience requires.

4 *Bildung* as a thoughtful disposition towards experience requires a reflective distancing from the immediacy of perception. To measure the everyday against the different demands acquiring the practice of "dealing with something that is not immediate, something that is alien, with something that belongs to memory and thought." This is not dealing with strangeness for strangeness' sake, but acquiring the preparedness to access the virtues of the foreign as a critical lever to challenge what lies in the expectancies of our own horizons.[26] Gadamer articulates the point in classical Hegelian terms: "to seek one's own in the alien, to become at home in it, is the basic movement of spirit, whose being is only return to itself from what is other." [27] Corollary 4: *Bildung* does not advocate a classical mode of education in and for itself. *Bildung* is not a disinterested academicism but intrinsically applicative. It concerns itself with establishing sanguine responses to the difficulties and demands of the present. Gadamer comments appropriately, "Learning does not mean learning to use a pre-existent tool for designating a world already somehow familiar to us: it means acquiring a familiarity and acquaintance with the world itself and how it confronts us."[28]

5 *Bildung* as capacity to act. *Bildung* fuses two channels of ethical praxis. Whereas Aristotle's concept of *catharsis* seeks to free human action from fearful inhibitions about the future, so *Bildung* attempts to develop a historical consciousness emboldening the contemporary mind not to be overwhelmed by the problems of immediacy. One response to such problems would be escapism, but *Bildung* is not aestheticist. Unlike Cartesian meditation which dwells on the unchanging underlying truths of appearance, hermeneutical reflection is closer to the Ignatian tradition which concerns itself with understanding what transcends yet informs the real, but precisely in order to intervene more effectively in the real. *Bildung* is essentially about enhancing such a capacity to act. Corollary 5: *Bildung* involves the practice of nurturing a disposition of poise which allows the mind a particular free mobility, moving back and forth between perceiving the whole in the part, and the part in the whole.

6 *Bildung* as tactfulness. *Bildung* involves a craftsmanlike "feeling and tact" from which the mind acquires a capacity for free mobility.[29] Gadamer writes, "By tact we understand a particular sensitivity and sensitiveness to situations, and how to behave in them, for which we cannot find any knowledge from general principles. Hence an essential part of tact is inexplicitness and inexpressibility."[30] The tact which functions in the human sciences is a mode both of knowing and of being.[31] That tact entails

"a trained receptivity towards otherness," understood either as the otherness of a work of art, of a remote historical culture, of the proximity of upheaval and change, or as an openness to other ways of doing and thinking. Corollary 6: the tactfulness of *Bildung* emphasizes its practical relation to aesthetics and aesthetic judgment. The reference to craftsman-like feeling concerns acquiring a feel for the material of a discipline, knowing how to find one's way within its horizons. Such a feeling, the sculptor's sense of the strengths and weaknesses of stone or the sailor's feel for the sea and its moods, is acquired by engaging in the concerns of a practice. Practices have their rules, but good practice is not a matter of blindly following them. The mariner "knows" what to do in a rising swell, but though his action may be rule-like, that is, derived from many years of experience, it is not the implementation of a pre-given rule. Cognitive judgments within the spheres of *Bildung* may exhibit the same logical order as aesthetic judgments of taste from prolonged practice of discernment. Practical experience inculcates a sense of both exemplary practice derived from the past and imaginatively projects where such a discipline might develop in the future. This illuminates two important points. (1) The freedom of action cherished by *Bildung* is not an *ex nihilo laissez-faire* conception, but is action with defining constraints. The response-repertoires to a contemporary social problematic are delimited by a knowledge of what exemplars from the past illuminate and inform the problematic in appropriate ways. Equally, a practitioner's knowledge of what informs his or her discipline strengthens a "feel" for response-repertoires in the challenging circumstances that the future inevitably brings. (2) The span between past precedent and future possibility that defines the constraining scope of possible action, sets the conceptual framework for answering our central question: can there be a philosophy of education which overreaches the transient? Philosophical hermeneutics promises an illuminating response to this question.

In summary, Gadamer's restatement of the classical doctrine of *Bildung* is not the repetition of a specific ideological commitment. It is a philosophical attempt to articulate a process of self-formation which neither depends on the self alone (it requires that a subject be ontologically placed in what is not self) nor culminates in a final self-image (*Bildung* involves the continual transformation and transcendence of the self). If there is a normative element to Gadamer's analysis, it lies in its status as a response to the following question: what mental disposition best befits an essenceless life-form in an ever changing environment? Given the ontological circumstances of such a life-form, any end goal for *Bildung* would be a contradiction in terms. It is clear, then, that the educative or formative element within *Bildung* has to do with achieving a maturity and intensity of response to the demands of a precarious form of existence.[32]

A Moving Experience

The connections between *Bildung*, formation, and those transformative responses to experience's challenge bind it to a certain phenomenological conception of the movement of thought and sensibility. Philosophical hermeneutics offers a compelling analysis of how such movement can be understood, and of how *Bildung* is both a consequence and an initiator of hermeneutical movements in understanding. There are at least three types of movement at play. (1) Social, cultural, and intellectual history all indicate that the subject matters of political and intellectual traditions are constantly shifting in content and nuance. (2) The meanings of a language constantly alter, reflecting changing social circumstances. (3) Individuals, family units or small social groupings generate shifts in local meaning and practice. None of these three types of movement are independent of each other. Indeed, the concept of *Bildung* requires that such different levels of meaning collide and moderate each other.

Gadamer's articulation of this key point is obtuse. In the essay "Hermeneutics and the Ontological Difference," the movement of seeing and thinking is likened to contemplative involvement with a subject matter: "In the puzzling miracle of mental wakefulness lies the fact that seeing something and thinking something are a kind of motion, but not the kind that leads from something to its end. Rather, when someone is looking at something, this is when he or she truly sees it, and when one is directing one's thinking at something, this is when he or she truly sees it, and when one is directing one's thinking at something, this is when one is truly pondering it. So motion is also a holding oneself in being, and through this motion of human wakefulness (*Wachseins*) there blows the whole breath of the life-process, a process that ever and again allows a new perception of something to open up."[33] The language of "truly" seeing and thinking does not intimate a fixity of essence to be grasped but, to the contrary, pondering and thinking involve a *becoming open to the movement in things*. As argued above, the formative process of *Bildung* does not commence *ex nihilo* but assumes that a hermeneutical subject is always already thrown into a certain cultural and linguistic horizon. Objects of contemplation are not so much physical entities but *Sachen*, culturally constituted thematics whose mode of being lies in the rhythm of their disclosures and withdrawals. Thinking and seeing in the above passage are not conceived instrumentally but aesthetically. *Bildung* involves nurturing the practice of seeing and thinking aesthetically, developing a contemplative disposition towards the movement *within* things. Openness to such movement is not a matter of detached observation but of informed participation: "this hermeneutical motion is also a holding oneself in being, and through this motion of human wakefulness, there blows the whole breath of life." Learning to be receptive to movements 1 and 2 (the movement within *Sachen* and different language traditions) is not an end in itself. It is, in effect, a tactical means to stimulate, induce, or trigger movement type 3 by placing our own hermeneutical horizons alongside those of other cultural groups. Movement 3 forms with movements 1 and 2 a hermeneutical double-helix. The semantic horizons of movements 1 and 2 effect a transformative change in movement 3, the result of which is a reconfiguration of one's immediate horizon of understanding. That reconfiguration in its turn forces changes in movements 1 and 2.

Let us grant in this connection that language works on many levels of meaning, that "things speak," and that *Sachen* have a language and, hence, multiple levels of meaning. Take, for example, the ordinary candle. It embodies a rich variety of meaning: a symbol of the fragility of the soul, a sign of spirituality and for those familiar with Max Beckman's painting *The Night*, an instrument of torture. A candle will reveal different aspects of its complex semantic field depending upon where and when it discloses itself. Artists know this. One expects candles to mark places of sacrifice or execution. One does not expect to see them flickering in a butcher's tray. Yet were one to see this, something more than an empty surreal gesture would be understood. How a *Sache* speaks, that is, what layer of meaning it discloses, depends on not just historical epoch or cultural style but on the specifics of location and circumstance. Gadamer emphasizes how it is the *Sache* that speaks through art. For the address to be understood presupposes a dialogical relation between a *Sache* and its addressee. Effective communication is not a matter of translating a determinant aspect of *Sache's* meaning to the mind of the spectator but rather of allowing that disclosure to trigger within the observer's response unexpected configurations of meaning and association. Just as the *Sache* has multiple layers of meaning, so too does the spectator's grasp of language and its own layers of personal nuance and application. Words have effective histories we do not control. We remain for the most part unaware of the sub-surface philological currents which both shape our mental shore-lines and always threaten to draw us into new cognitive waters. An unaccustomed juxtaposition of words, a novel locution, an accidental remark can suddenly breech the mental and social dykes of habit which channel the movement of customary usages of meaning. What itself moves (the rhythmic disclosures of the subject matter associated with movements 1 and 2), moves us (stimulates the emergence of new associations of meaning as in movement 3), which in turn serves through continued dialogical participation to "move along" the cultural dialogue which grounds the possibility of collective transformation and transcendence.

We have now described what is in effect the formative movement of *Bildung*. In summary: 1. *Bildung* does not take place *ex nihilo*, but ontologically presupposes that all human beings are located in and shaped by cultural and linguistic traditions (movements 1 and 2 above). 2. *Bildung* entails the practice of taking an explicit degree of autonomous control over that implicit process. 3. Becoming *gebildet* is knowing how to put oneself in the way of the movement within *Sachen* precisely in order to be questioned, challenged, and potentially transformed by such engagement and interaction. 4. The person who is *gebildet* is an "experienced" intellectual traveler who has gained not so much knowledge but a heightened sensibility concerning what is needed in the face of continuous hermeneutical change and exchange. 5. *Bildung* is a continuous practice, a respectful and careful disposition towards the genuine complexities of experience; it is, in effect, a "moving," very human "way" of being.

The English political philosopher Michael Oakeshott offers a description of a dialogical mode of education which provides an apt conclusion to this more analytical aspect of our discussion of *Bildung*: "Education, properly speaking, is an initiation into the skill and partnership of this conversation which, in the end, gives place and character to every human activity and utterance, and in which we acquire the intellectual and moral habits appropriate to conversation. And it is this conversation which in the end gives place and character to every human activity and utterance. I say, 'in the end,' because of course the immediate end of moral activity is the world of practical enterprise, and intellectual achievement appears, in the first place, within each of the various universes of discourse; but good behaviour is what it is with us because practical enterprise is recognised not as an isolated activity but as a partner in a conversation, and the final measure of intellectual achievement is in terms of its contribution to the conversation in which all universes of discourse meet."[34]

Echoes: Humanist Reformations

Gadamer is not alone in his defense of *Bildung* as a transformative educational process. If continuing historical disclosures of hidden determinations of meaning from within a concept mark its profundity and continuing relevance, the resurgence of interest in the notion of *Bildung* confirms what Gadamer would call its historical effectiveness. Michael Oakeshott presents *Bildung* as being geared primarily towards a freedom of action "unfettered by coercion or by compulsive desires . . . and informed by reflective appraisal of the choices available."[35] Freedom is not understood as an unspecified liberal ideal but as the ability not to be overwhelmed by the needs of circumstance. It responds to those needs with the skill and confidence acquired from meeting the challenges of long experience. In Oakeshott's view a liberal education is *liberating* in that it presupposes breaking free from "the distracting business of satisfying contingent human wants."[36] This accords with Gadamer's account of the value of "hermeneutical" seeing, that is, paying attention to things (*Sachen*) in their own right rather than according to the dictates of interest. Oakeshott also emphasizes that *Bildung* is not a heroic individualist enterprise but one which depends upon open converse among persons. *Bildung* is interactive and cannot "be pursued in the isolation of a self-reflective intelligence but depends on the enquiries and actions in which others have expressed their understanding of the human condition." [37] Lars Lovlie and Paul Standish argue that "such a process of discovery cannot take place in abstraction but requires the learner to come to recognise 'some *specific* invitations to encounter *particular* adventures in human self-understanding.'"[38] In its encounter with particular works or traditions of enquiry "such education cannot but be culturally embedded. . . . This is an intellectual and a moral inheritance." For Oakeshott, "there is no other way for a human being to make the most of himself than by learning to recognise himself in the mirror of this inheritance."[39]

Sven Nordenbo emphasizes the participatory element of *Bildung*: a person has acquired *Bildung* only if he or she has assisted *actively* in its formation or development.[40] This emphasizes the anti-essentialism associated with the concept of *Bildung*. Mortensen argues that "the self is seen as a reflexive project, for which the individual is responsible. . . . We are, not what we are, but what we make of ourselves."[41] This self-creating act is retrospective: "what the individual becomes is dependent on the reconstructive endeavours in which he or she engages."[42] But it is also prospective: "Identity is a project."[43] Nevertheless, such a project is fundamentally a dialogical achievement. Neo-humanist *Bildung* theory insists that "a person who develops without contact with the world has no relation to objectivity. A person who subjects himself to the world's demands for usefulness loses his individuality. With such an educational theory, neo-humanist *Bildung* theory tries to preserve the individual in the objective and the objective in the individual."[44] *Bildung* involves the public or objective sphere being internalized by the individual who is led thereby from subjective belief to objective knowledge or wisdom: insight into the historical terms of one's own insight is also insight into the objective world.[45] A feature of that world is its constituting tensions.

Sven Nordenbo argues that the formative process of *Bildung* embraces a tension between the imperatives of individual development and those of *Herrschaft* (power and governance). *Bildung* is primarily concerned with persons developing according to the dynamic of their interests in contrast to society which for its part wishes to shape individuals with its needs. Although *Bildung* is initially grounded in local practices and perspectives, being responsive to the claims of social culture will inevitably undermine traditional upbringing. Nevertheless, the social or collective claim is always moderated and challenged by the primary subjectivity of the individual—a kind of spontaneity that challenges the powers of normalization and convention. In this connection Gert Biesta observes that the aim of critical *Bildung* is to decipher the operations of power behind what presents itself as necessary, natural, general, and universal.[46] As Ilan Gur-ze'ev notes, this is what makes *Bildung* so attractive to Horkheimer and Adorno: *Bildung* as education is not to be reduced to mere cultivation or socialization but can serve as an immanent critique of moral and political norms.[47] Thus, Helmut Peukert contends that *Bildung* does not involve the mere appropriation of inherited knowledge but should be understood as the ability to go beyond the present state of affairs and to transform the structures and prevailing rules of current life.[48]

The political implications of the anti-essentialist dimensions of *Bildung* are taken up by Ronald Reichenback who contends that, ideally, members of democratic forms of living must reckon from the beginning with self-deception. *Herrschaft* and other normalizing forces attempt to persuade the individual that he or she has a determinate nature. Philosophical hermeneutics denies the identity thesis and emphasizes after Hoelderlin that whatever we are results from "the conversation that we are." Whatever self-knowledge we have is limited and provisional. In democratic forms of living, members should never "forget" themselves, that is, always assume the *possibility* of self-deception which, in hermeneutical terms, means remaining vigilant about assuming neither the completeness nor universality of one's cognitive outlook.[49]

These recent approaches to the concept of *Bildung* may not have the solid ontological grounding which philosophical hermeneutics provides, but they demonstrate the continuing relevance of the concept. Gadamer's "radical orthodoxy" with regard to *Bildung* and its entailments is neither as reactionary nor as eccentric as sometimes suggested. The theoretical case for the continuing relevance of *Bildung* is robust. What of the practical case? Hard-nosed instrumentalist calls for the tailoring of educational policy to economic need are not to be refuted by nostalgic calls for better or more rounded persons. Instrumentalism must be fought with instrumentalist arguments. The case for *Bildung* and its transformative approach to education comes into its own.

The Power of the Useless or "How Philosophy can (indeed) be useful for the benefit of the people"![50]

In certain forms of art, actuality is reconstructed according to a work's internal logic. Occasionally, the world seems to reconstruct itself according to the logic of an art work. Kafka's novel *The Castle* offers a prescient image of the darkness at the heart of contemporary government. Spreading economic freedom and the deregulation it encourages creates an increasing dependence upon "the center." Communities are now "free" to anxiously pursue the best insurance scheme or mortgage investment. Rather than liberating individuals from everyday needs, economic freedoms create more time for people to become evermore dependent upon the prevailing system. The shadows of Kafka's castle walls have lengthened. Institutionalized centers seem to maintain themselves by generating uncertainty. Stupidity and dependency have been instrumentalized and education reduced to attend market demands. This is education for redundancy.

Instrumentalization assumes (1) market stability, (2) a predictability of need, and (3) market dominance. All three assumptions are notoriously fragile. (1) Markets are only stable if energy prices are non-volatile. Yet the politics of the Near East has profoundly changed Western market stability. (2) Needs can disappear as easily as they emerge. Consider the impact computerization made upon market demand for office space. (3) Market dominance can only be sustained by a knowledge monopoly, but prevalent technologies are notoriously unpredictable as to their future relevance. In short, the instrumentalist thesis is wedded to maintaining the status quo economically and, hence, promotes cyclical redundancy. To respond only to present need merely invests in the transience of the immediate. An instrumentalist educational policy which seeks to address pressing needs alone in fact promotes redundancy. An educational policy emphasizing the formative capacity of *Bildung* promotes a variety of reactions to contemporary challenges mobilizing an altogether more diverse and flexible historical and cultural vocabulary of response. *Bildung* offers a better long-term survival investment.

The advantage of the *Bildung* argument is that it sensitizes individuals to what is happening in fields other than their own. Understanding voices shaped by world-outlooks other than our own is not an indulgent exercise in accommodating strangeness. A formidable obstacle to creativity concerns the often comfortable, imaginative blinkering associated with ends-related thinking. The convenience of habitual assumptions is powerful. *Bildung* understood as a responsive analytic and critical practice counteracts such complacent ease. The acquaintance with the strange, other, and foreign challenges the narrowness of the habitual. A consciousness shaped by *Bildung* is not hemmed in by the immediate and transient but extends a community of dialogue to include those who stand well beyond the known and immediate. The impromptu consequences of such dialogue reveal something of the distinct character of education in the humanities: though it is impossible to predict the precise outcome of such dialogue, it would be injudicious not to invest in the likelihood of a positive serendipitous impact somewhere and at sometime within one or other discipline. A person who is *gebildet* acquires patient confidence in the future: experience teaches that game-changing insights often emerge from outside a discipline. The practice of wide reading in the humanities is no more a liberal luxury than reading military history is a mere entertainment for the soldier. Both teach the lessons of spiritual short-sightedness and calcified imaginations and both extend repertoires of response to envisage future difficulties. An education in hermeneutics, philosophy, or theology may not seem relevant to a hard-pressed economist. Hard-headed instrumentalism suggests otherwise. High ratings of employment for graduates in these disciplines suggest that open-minded flexibility is a skill with a market premium. "Useless?" An education in the humanities requires an ability to grapple with the logical structure of complex problems, to review unfamiliar ideas with an open mind, to acquire the patience of listening and for long-term reflection, and to examine issues in a multi-perspectival way. This much was rediscovered during the oil-related economic downturns of the late 1960s and early 1970s. Does history now repeat itself? Perhaps, only for those who have not learned its lessons.

What proves to be of significant and historical value in humanities research can be a consequence of maintaining the momentum of a research practice rather than of the pursuit of a predefined goal. What matters is not singular devotion to a method but the willingness to engineer methodically those circumstances in or between disciplines that induce those *eureika* moments capable of transforming an understanding of a problem. The encouragement of education and research with no obvious outcome may, in the present climate of severe financial restraint, seem fanciful. Yet it is precisely such pursuits that encourage the creativity and poise required for confronting contemporary social and economic difficulties. If a living system is not to wither in the shadow of Kafka's castle then, as Varela contends, it must continually bring the significant experiences and concepts that form its self-understanding under review. Hermeneutics is the discipline par excellence which fulfills such critical distance. It facilitates the broad transmission and exchange of ideas. A community incapable of exposing itself to the risks and challenges of such exchange has little hope of prospering. For that exchange to be of consequence, then, as Gadamer argues, free spaces for transformative reflection are needed. The promotion of *Bildung* in persons and institutions establishes such spaces. Their instrumental justification lies not in the scholarly work produced but in what the practices (which sustain that work) enable beyond the individual researcher, that is, the production of those serendipitous impacts and effects that can genuinely transform the understanding and creativity of individuals and communities.

And so?

Philosophical hermeneutics and *Bildung* are not synonymous and yet each demands the other. Hermeneutics must by default advocate the formative practice which is *Bildung* as without it hermeneutics could not itself be practiced. The end of philosophical hermeneutics is to engender those modes of dialogical engagements with texts which allow them to speak, and yet the maneuvering and manipulation of methods deployed to that end require a poise and tacit know-how which can only be acquired by the practice of hermeneutics. *Bildung* is not itself hermeneutics, but the effect of that practice.

Bildung is formative. It is not ends-related. If it were, it would be of limited instrumentalist use since the pursuit of a specific or immediate end is of transient value. *Bildung* is formative as it concerns the development of a wide but highly focusable response capacity to cultural challenges of a social or economic order. This is the instrumental value of *Bildung*. Thus, philosophical hermeneutics establishes a conception education (formations) which is neither essentialist nor merely an opportunist acquiescence to ever-changing political agendas. The merit of this conception is that it overreaches the transient precisely because of its emphasis on the formative. Recent defenses of the humanities have not served *Bildung* well. Reticence in the face of postmodern critiques of humanism has led to an embarrassing silence as to what it is about humanity that the humanities serve.[51] Yet Varela, Vattimo and Gadamer avoid privileging the human by insisting that the question of what humanity is resides in keeping that question open. An attractive feature of philosophical hermeneutics' defense of formative *Bildung* is its congruence with that anthropological ontology which contends that the bios of the human is to be in motion, that is, to have the capacity for constant innovation and transformation. More embarrassing are the arguments which defend the humanities as ends in themselves. Philosophical hermeneutics is more pragmatic. To appeal to something for its own sake suggests that it stands outside all relations. Hermeneutics insists that an object independent of cognitive relations has no relevance to life phenomenologically conceived. When Gadamer adopts the language of aesthetic (disinterested) seeing he is not appealing to the quietist aestheticism of seeing things in themselves but to opening towards the movement in things (*Sachen*) which everyday goal-orientated perception prevents us from seeing. But not even this is the point. Putting ourselves in the way of the movement of things (*Sachen*) allows that movement to induce further movement in how we see those objects and what is related to them. This is the instrumentalist justification of *Bildung*. That cognitive movement takes us beyond the immediate issue or problem (sets a reflective distance between ourselves and it). It allows us to see its hermeneutical provenance as well as its possible future determinations. That movement is therefore capable of transforming our understanding of the question at issue. In conclusion, *Bildung* centers upon and is the effective and affective consequence of individual hermeneutical practice. It concerns the acquisition of a pragmatic and instrumental skill, the ability to see in each present difficulty the traces of its history and the promise of future alternative interpretive responses. Such poise expresses a commendable and very human virtue, not to be unsettled or disappointed by the inevitability of change, but rather to be open to the hermeneutical opportunities for transformation that it holds. In so far as *Bildung* is an effect of its practice, philosophical hermeneutics offers an education for all seasons.

Notes

1 John Cottingham, *On the Meaning of Life* (London: Routledge, 2003), 100.
2 *The Oxford Dictionary of English Etymology* (London: Clarendon Press, 1976).

[3] Wilhelm von Humboldt, *The Limits of State Action*, ed. J. W. Burrow (London: Cambridge University Press, 1969), xviii–xix.
[4] Hans-Georg Gadamer, *Truth and Method* (London: Sheed and Ward, 1989), xxxiii.
[5] W. Humboldt, *The Limits of State Action*, xx.
[6] Ernst Cassirer, *An Essay on Man*, cited in Ernst Cassirer, *The Philosophy of Symbolic Forms* (London: Yale University Press, 1980), 7.
[7] Gianni Vattimo, *Nihilism and Emancipation: Ethics, Politics, and Law*, ed. Santiago Zabala, trans. William McCuaig (New York: Columbia University Press, 2004), 36.
[8] Gianni Vattimo with R. Rorty. *The Future of Religion*, ed. Santiago Zabala (New York: Columbia University Press, 2005), 3.
[9] Ibid., 4.
[10] Henri Frankfort, *Before Philosophy: The Intellectual Adventure of Ancient Man* (Baltimore: Penguin Books, 1971), 243.
[11] Friedrich Nietzsche, *The Will to Power* (London: Weidenfeld and Nicolson, 1980), section 585.
[12] Gadamer, *Truth and Method*, 318.
[13] Ibid., 318.
[14] Ibid., xxx.
[15] Ibid., 319.
[16] Wolfgang Iser, *The Range of Interpretation* (New York: Columbia University Press, 2000), 101.
[17] Ibid., 105.
[18] John Shotter, "Co-creating Innovative Developments in a Practice from within the Practice: a Corporeal Approach to Overcoming Orientational Difficulties," a paper presented at the University of St. Andrews, Scotland, on November 2009, 3 (unpublished).
[19] Iser, *The Range of Interpretation* 105.
[20] Ibid., 105.
[21] Nietzsche, *The Will to Power*, section 635.
[22] Herder speaks of formation (*Bildung*) as rising "out of the most particular individual need and returned back to it—pure experience, action, life-application in the most defined circle" (Herder, *Philosophical Writings*, ed. Michael Forster [London: Cambridge University Press, 2002], 323). Hegel famously extends formation to the universal development of mind (*Geist*). See Allen Wood, "Hegel on Education," in *Philosophy of Education*, ed. Amelie Rorty (London: Routledge, 1998).
[23] Gadamer, *Truth and Method*, 13.
[24] Ibid., 11.
[25] Ibid., 12.
[26] Ibid., 14.
[27] Ibid., 15.
[28] Gadamer, *Philosophical Hermeneutics*, ed. D. Linge (Berkeley: University of California Press, 1976), "Man and Language of Things," 69–81.
[29] Gadamer, *Truth and Method*, 16.
[30] Ibid., 17.
[31] Ibid., 17.
[32] See Nicholas Davey, *Unquiet Understanding* (Albany: State University of New York Press).
[33] *The Gadamer Reader*, ed. Richard E. Palmer (Evanston: Illinois University Press, 2007), 367.
[34] Michael Oakeshott, *Rationalism in Politics and Other Essays* (London: Methuen, 1981), 198.
[35] *Journal of Philosophy of Education* 36 (3), August 2002, 330.
[36] *Journal of Philosophy of Education*36 (3), August 2002, 28.
[37] *Journal of Philosophy of Education* 36 (3), August 2002, 331.
[38] Ibid.
[39] Ibid.
[40] *Journal of Philosophy of Education* 36 (3), August 2002, 341.
[41] *Journal of Philosophy of Education* 36 (3), August 2002, 441.
[42] Ibid.
[43] Ibid.
[44] *Journal of Philosophy of Education* 36 (3), August 2002, 351.
[45] *Journal of Philosophy of Education* 36 (3), August 2002, 350.

[46] *Journal of Philosophy of Education* 36 (no. 3), August 2002, 383.
[47] *Journal of Philosophy of Education* 36 (3), August 2002, 391, 404.
[48] *Journal of Philosophy of Education,* 36 (3), August 2002, 422.
[49] *Journal of Philosophy of Education* 36 (3), August 2002, 417–18.
[50] Herder, *Philosophical Writings,* ed. Michael Forster (London: Cambridge University Press, 2002), 25.
[51] Matthew Reizz, "Beyond Measure? Fears for Humanities' Future in an Impact-Driven Academy," *The Times Higher Education Supplement,* January 7, 2010, 32–7.

Chapter 4

The Education of the Teacher

Graeme Nicholson

There have been many kinds of hermeneutical theory, and all of them have close ties to education. In the early modern period, legal and theological hermeneutics were sketched out as auxiliary disciplines for the work of the university faculties of law and theology. In the nineteenth century, Schleiermacher and Dilthey widened the scope of hermeneutics, but it was still focused on texts and the interpretation of them as practiced by scholars and teachers. Heidegger and Gadamer deepened the discipline further to reach right into the movement of our existence, and while their hermeneutics does not betray an academic character quite so evidently, the educational dimension remains essential to it nevertheless. It is not the array of differentiated faculties and the institutional division of school and university that interests them, but rather questions that are extremely fundamental. How can scholarship truly bring us understanding? How can science truly bring us knowledge? They ask: What must happen to the pupil, what must happen to the teacher, if the two of them are indeed to understand and know their subjects?

Central to Heidegger's *Being and Time* is the theme of disclosure: our being in the world is guided by an understanding that is disclosive, for we project meanings that allow things to show themselves to us.[1] This event of interpretation is co-extensive with human existence, and is illuminated by our being (*BT*, 350–1). Philosophy explains the understanding, interpretation, and truth that everyone lives through all the time, and so it is the original form of hermeneutics. Understanding and disclosure afford the basis for textual interpretation, and they are also what make education possible. The illumination of our existence makes us able to learn, and the disclosures accomplished by understanding constitute our knowledge. Being with others is also primordial in our existence, so that mutual understanding through discourse belongs to us all. Clearly, education is one of the master varieties of our being with one another.

Gadamer's *Truth and Method* (a text that Heidegger himself came increasingly to appreciate with the passing years) is complementary to *BT* in both respects, both as an account of truth centered on disclosure and as an account of education.[2] It treats hermeneutics by starting with truth in Part One (i.e., disclosure), understanding in Part Two, and language in Part Three. Gadamer keeps education clearly in view throughout the book. Truth, especially as manifested in the work of art, is nothing without the receptiveness of each new generation. The principal condition for understanding is the history that mediates a work to us through explanation, imitation, and scholarship. Hermeneutics finds its real-world setting in the practice of education.

Both Heidegger and Gadamer seek to avoid the status of revolutionaries or innovators. In *BT*, p. 19, we read, "Whether the [account] is 'novel' is of no importance and remains extrinsic. What is positive . . . must lie in the fact that it is *old* enough to enable us to learn to comprehend the possibilities prepared by the 'ancients.'" Gadamer stresses his indebtedness, for instance, to Plato and Aristotle, with books, chapters, and essays stressing how much the classical texts have to teach us about the business of hermeneutics. The dialogical style of Plato is a model for our encounter with texts (*TM*, pp. 344–60); the ethics of practical wisdom, *phronēsis*, in Aristotle is not only a guide to action but also to reading (*TM*, pp. 295–307); the humanism of the post-Renaissance period offers Gadamer insights into literary criticism, right in the opening chapter of *TM*. If there is one common point evident in these historical excurses, it is that all of them concern education in one way or another. Platonic dialogue was an educational practice, and so were the ethics of Aristotle, and so was the "criticism" of the humanists. Even if we had no other evidence of the educational dimension of hermeneutics, the historical references would make it plain as day.

In the first part of this chapter, I shall show some of the positive contributions that, according to Gadamer, the humanist tradition has made to hermeneutical inquiry, emphasizing the idea of education (*Bildung*) that accompanies humanism. As the chapter develops, I shall try to show some beneficial implications we can derive from this idea. I shall sketch the kind of university that was originally associated with *Bildung* and then explore to what extent this *Bildung* is still available in our universities and schools. *Bildung* is an education in *thinking*.

What I am stressing above all is the person, the existence, and the education (*Bildung*) of the *teacher*. Though the primary school teacher and the post-secondary teacher could certainly be imagined here, it is especially the high school teacher that is at the forefront of my attention.

The Idea of *Bildung*

Gadamer inaugurates his account of hermeneutics by citing some antecedents or prototypes from the humanist tradition of post-Renaissance Europe. Teachers and scholars cultivated rhetoric and classical studies, and both the family and the school sought to develop in young people a taste for art and literature and a capacity to judge excellence in the arts. Along with this, there were many reflections about the proper norms for reading. It is not surprising that there has long been an informal culture that offers substantial insights into arts and letters, along with the criticism and interpretation of them. After all, we all take an interest in works of art and literature, and have some sense of the history of our country and the world in advance of any rigorous study of the humanities. Though Gadamer will not rest with the humanist tradition, it affords him some guidelines that will eventually be integrated into his complete hermeneutical theory. Good judgment and good taste were traditionally praised as the kind of discernment that recognizes excellence and beauty in works of art: Gadamer cites especially Gracian's theory of *gusto* (pp. 31–9). Taste and judgment cannot be taught out of books, and they proceed without following rules; they are always aimed at the singular work, and do not "deduce" a judgment logically out of universal principles. Yet good taste is a cognitive power. Because it is fused with sensation (*Empfindung*), it preserves a kinship with the physical tasting of the tongue.

In humanism, these qualities or gifts were linked with the *sensus communis*: a *common* faculty dwelling in the mind that was not yet specialized into the diverse sense modalities and the intellect (a sort of mental stem cell). Vico especially (*TM*, pp. 16–27) praised this as the quality that is cultivated by rhetoric, poetry, epic, and history, and that is generally ruined by too much mathematics, physics, and logic. For Gadamer, therefore, Vico's studies were a true prototype of hermeneutics. The *sensus communis* cultivated by literary and historical study is precisely the power that attains the true understanding of works of art and poetry, and it lies behind good judgment and good taste. This humanist tradition manifested resistance to the dominance of "science," that is, the axiomatic, mathematical, physical investigation of nature, a resistance personified in Vico's critique of Descartes. But we may note *en passant* that when hermeneutics is fully developed by Gadamer into a philosophical form, it will not leave the domain of mathematical and natural science untouched, for it will show how these sciences, like all experience, incorporate understanding and interpretation into their very fabric.[3]

In Gadamer's opening review of the humanist tradition, all these virtues become linked with another idea that was developed especially in Germany—an educational program that they called *Bildung*. Gadamer even calls *Bildung* the greatest idea of the eighteenth century (*WM*, 7). If we translate this term as "formation," it must be with caution, for it cannot be understood as the imposition of form upon the plastic soul. Nor can *Bildung* be understood as a "cultivation" that permits the hidden talents of the soul to come forth and be manifest. Though it sounds like the English "build," the word has a different root, stemming from *Bild*, meaning effigy, likeness, picture. The engraving of a portrait on a coin is an example of *bilden*, and in our *Bildung* such a picture is communicated to us. Gadamer stresses the double meaning of *Bild* that can be both *Vorbild*, the model or prototype, and *Nachbild*, the copy or likeness (*WM*, 8). This point is vitally important, and we shall return to it below.

It was Johann Gottfried Herder who, in the 1770s, proclaimed the ideal of a *Bildung der Menschheit* (forming of humanity) as a *Empor-Bildung zur Menschheit* (raising up *to* humanity) (*TM*, 7). That was one expression of the forceful driving movement in Germany, the *Sturm und Drang* that opposed the rationalists' Enlightenment ideal that human beings should perfect themselves. Rather, we need to strive first to *become* human. Herder's pamphlets were to serve both for the renewal of the nation and as an ideal for the education of the individual.[4] As this ideal spread in the post-Kantian generation, it was realized as a collective and reflexive project, *Sich-bilden*, where everyone was at once both "forming" and "formed." The implication that Gadamer stresses is that all connections with a naturalistic shaping and forming were now broken: Wilhelm von Humboldt expressed the contrast of *Bildung* with *Kultur* as something higher and more inward (*TM*, 8). The connection with the earlier humanistic tradition is, of course, that this post-Kantian generation understood that judgment, taste, and even *sensus communis* were to be *gebildet*—they were not just talents of the individual to be "cultivated," but rather they became the substance of public education.

Gadamer highlights three elements: (1) *Bildung* is what affords a sense of the "other," the "foreign," even in its particularity. Of course, the mastery of languages, the study of world literatures, and anthropology were to become major emphases of German education in this period. Therefore, Hegel especially understood *Bildung* as the attainment of the universal, which here meant one's growing out of immediacy and particularity, for example, German provinciality. (2) *Bildung* is the very element in which spirit exists; spirit is never merely given, existing naturally, but exists only in the process of self-forming and becoming: "by nature we are not what we ought to be, and need *Bildung*" (9). For Hegel, as Gadamer stresses, the life of spirit *is* that exiting from private existence that can encounter the other and then return to itself. (3) All this takes place essentially in the social medium of the whole people, and relies upon an experience of memory that is trans-individual: for Hegel, classical studies were the world-historical exercise of memory that quite outreached the individual consciousness. But this memory too must be *gebildet.*

It is not difficult to see the relevance of this idea to the whole development of German scholarship in the nineteenth century, and to the problem of hermeneutics as Gadamer poses it in his book. It is the one who is *gebildet* who is able to understand and interpret. A *Bildung* through language-study and literature is a good illustration of the special features of this memory. Gadamer mentions (*TM*, 9) the use of grammar books and books of excerpts which are employed to help us master a language. These materials are usually abandoned once their function has been performed. We also study literary works as we advance in our language studies—but these are not destined to be abandoned as our understanding of the language progresses. Such poems and essays become the permanent possession of the person who has received this *Bildung.* Our entire thought world, our memory, has been extended. This shows that language study is not really a technical discipline, leading to a technical mastery of a language. This is the educational aspect of literature and it should not be overly aestheticized, for that can immunize us to the appeal that the work addresses to us: what it says, how it speaks. A critique of Schiller's *Letters on the Aesthetic Education of Man* is one of the climactic passages in *TM*, Part One: we read that this classic text has tended to turn literary education into a school for the precious and the genteel.[5]

Humboldtian Education

(a) *Berlin.* The exceptional interest of this idea of *Bildung* is that it did not remain merely a pedagogical and epistemological idea, but was central in the reform of German education in the early years of the nineteenth century. Fichte, von Humboldt, and others put this project to work especially in the foundation of the University of Berlin in 1810. We can see that this educational practice bore great fruit all through nineteenth-century Germany, with the flourishing of scholarship, philology, linguistics, anthropology—not to mention the natural sciences. Much of the inspiration was due to von Humboldt, whose own linguistic studies came to embrace all the continents of the globe, just as his brother Alexander traversed the whole world as an adventurer and anthropologist. Wilhelm von Humboldt was a literary scholar, writing critical studies of Goethe and other poets, and a linguist, the true founder of the comparative science of linguistics. He was also Minister of Education in the government of Prussia, and his educational interests were by no means confined to the university. He reformed the entire school system of Prussia, and his writings on language exhibit his deep interest in the language and thought of the child. He stresses very strongly the spontaneity, individuality, and autonomy of the human soul, especially the child, and he is "careful to separate the idea of *Bildung*, education which develops the whole individual, from the concept of vocational training, education which develops a specific skill."[6]

Here we can review another publication by Gadamer that gives a very clear idea of the aims and achievements of the "Humboldtian" university.[7] This new institution was conceived to be different from the universities that had grown up in Europe during and after the Middle Ages, for theirs had had an orthodox style of instruction conceived as the passing on to a new generation of what was known, what Gadamer calls *doctrina* (47–8). This new university was not founded on *doctrina* but on research (*Forschung*): the students were to be exposed to the research activity of the professors, what Humboldt phrased as "science which has not yet been completely discovered." The students could become exposed to the borderline between what had been discovered and the looming darkness of the unknown. Of course, a fair part of this education would encompass some catching up, some learning of what *had* been discovered hitherto, but this was preparatory to the pursuit of hitherto unsolved questions. This *Bildung* was not defined as preparation for a profession. Of course, every student awaited a future life in the exercise of some profession: medicine, law, teaching, but the research undertaken in the course of *Bildung* was not supposed to have anything to do with that ultimate profession. The future physician was to be *gebildet* through the study, for instance, of Assyriology, with some participation in the preparation of an Assyrian lexicon. "What Humboldt wished to denote with this word [*Bildung*] was not opposition to the uneducated, but . . . against developing the university into a professional school. It meant, therefore, opposition to the expert [*Fachmann*]" (48). The student's life was conceived as quite detached from social obligations, to the end of "living with ideas." What made this possible, for Humboldt, was a student's existence in solitude and freedom. "The freedom to structure one's studies and the solitude of research were the important founding values of this idea of the university" (48). Humboldt believed that the *learned* [*gebildet*] professions—medicine, law, the church—would thereby become infused with the honesty and doubt that always pertain to research undertaken with utmost seriousness. It was this experience, not the content, that constituted *Bildung*, and the graduate would take away this idea of education. Gadamer interprets this ideal, perhaps more radically than Humboldt himself, as opening upon an infinite horizon of thinking and questioning: "A never-ending process of learning occurs which does not end in knowledge. To remain incomplete is the fate of our desire to learn and know." (56)

In the second half of this section, I want to ponder what this ideal of education might mean for someone who is to embark upon the teaching profession, especially in a high school. Does this idea of *Bildung* offer us any positive insights for our own educational practice? After all, Humboldt himself was as interested in public schools as he was in the university. What about the possibility of a "science that has not yet been completely discovered"? An exposure to this can certainly stir the mind and imagination of a student, with the most varied consequences. This is precisely what we call "thinking" in the emphatic sense. Such an exposure counterweighs the course of studies that prepares a candidate for entry into one of the professions: it opens the mind to the vast field of possible intellectual work. The physician who has been exposed to Assyriology and the preparation of a lexicon will be less ready, in the future, to acquiesce in the conventions that pertain to the normal practices of the profession. Moreover, the continuing effect of such a *Bildung* is a *Sich-bilden*, a reflexive self-education that is likely to be lifelong. As we shall see in the concluding section, the heart of the experience is the discovery of the *Vorbild*, that criterion of truth that constitutes every education, even the education that one practices upon oneself.

(b) *Thinking.* North American universities incorporate the principle that research and teaching are carried on in the same institutions and departments, and by the same academics. Although critics sometimes claim that faculty research diverts too much time and attention away from teaching, the usual reply is that the professors' research strengthens their teaching. Let us explore this reply.

There are several kinds of cases. First, a professor can acquaint students with the current specialized research in his or her field, including of course research carried on elsewhere. This is especially appropriate with senior students and graduate students who are apprenticing as scholars. But we wonder whether such a *Bildung* could have further applications among undergraduates at a lower level. Is there a place here for "science that has not yet been completely discovered"? Let us note that there are many courses in which an instructor is operating fairly far from home base, the field of his or her specialized research, offering instruction in a field which he or she is *still learning*, ideally not utterly remote from the primary field of research but cognate to some degree. What this teacher has is not field-specific expertise but rather an experience with research and teaching that brings a capacity to seek and to learn, and a greater skill than most students have in formulating questions. These courses are exceptionally valuable, and in the nature of things there are many of them. What the students witness in such a course is the *Sich-bilden*, the self-education, of their teacher, and in this communication they can acquire a sense of how this is done. We can contrast their experience with another in which a university appoints senior professors to teach introductory courses, with the hope of "authoritative lectures" by a "leading expert." This *can* have a bad effect on younger students (not always, of course), encouraging dogmatism.

Moreover, while today's academic atmosphere may not be as austere and creative as that of von Humboldt's Berlin, we must recognize that universities are full of new scholarly initiatives—to mention just one, the application of social science to the life sciences and physical sciences—and many courses offered in this spirit are exploratory; with "science that has not yet been completely discovered," students and faculty educate themselves together.

Moreover, students are usually encouraged to take courses outside their own immediate field of specialization, and they can often excel in them, more than specialists, for reasons similar to the case of the teacher who is still learning. Like the professor who is still learning, these students are engaged in "extraneous research," as I shall call it (outside the specialty), though it is research carried on in connection with some course of instruction. These too are cases of "science that is not yet completely discovered." Like Humboldt, I am of course presupposing that this student does possess some research specialization. The student doing an outside minor in another discipline can form some idea of that discipline as a whole, vague and partial to be sure, but still one that can challenge the views of the "insiders" up to a point. An economics student, enrolled in a literature course, will perhaps raise the question of the economic foundations of English poetry. Besides that, this excursion to the outside can open up some further understanding of one's home discipline (this economics student may now be led to wonder, critically, why mathematics is so prevalent in economics). That professor that we imagined, teaching a subject that he or she was still learning, was also once a student, and did an "outside minor" in the same way, and, besides that, is always encountering other disciplines at faculty meetings. We all form rough general ideas of all disciplines, our own and the other ones as well. It is our sense of the "disciplines," not the specific courses, that will concern me in the rest of the chapter.

We are now going to follow this university student into the vocation of high school teaching. It makes a great deal of difference to a teacher's work what kind of university education he or she has had. We are altogether too prone in our civilization to attribute a teacher's excellences to personality, character, and innate intelligence, overlooking that intellectual component of excellent teaching that stems from the teacher's own education. In the appraisal of university preparation, I mean to lay stress on the "outside minor," and on the "science that has not yet been completely discovered." For these are valuable stimuli to a power that is extraordinarily valuable to a high school teacher: that of self-education. Having become acquainted with the self-education of one's own teachers at university endows one with a gift for this oneself. It is communicated.

Teachers are generally expected to have degree-level competence in the discipline of instruction, yet they often branch out into one or more other subjects. This point is important for my argument, not because I wish to say one cannot teach one's own subject well, but for another reason. The quality that *permits* a teacher to branch out is a general intellectual endowment that also shows up when one instructs in one's own subject. That power that enables a teacher to "get up" an unfamiliar subject also enables the teacher to entertain new approaches to his or her own subject, and to experiment with ideas. It is the teacher's quality of mind that is under discussion here: I am offering a picture of the *thinking teacher*. This quality is important above all because it can become communicated—to high school students.

The high school has a curriculum defining bodies of knowledge that are to be transmitted to the students. Obviously the teaching staff needs to cover that curriculum. But in addition to covering a body of knowledge, a high school course has the further possibility of awakening the mind of the student. This is no small supplement to the "real work" of education; it is just as germane to education as covering the material. That is why I want to focus on the thinking teacher. One factor that makes a difference, I believe, is the self-education of the teacher. The exposure to "science that is not yet completely discovered" is an entrée to the lifelong self-education of the teacher.

Thinking can be concerned with absolutely any subject matter (not only philosophical topics): properties of bodies, questions of laws and rights, poetry, and so on. In any course of instruction the teacher has an opportunity for communicating his or her thinking, and it can have remarkable effects. Consider a history teacher who is offering instruction in Canadian history. If the teacher has read documents of the nineteenth century, and current documents and research, he or she has had to ponder whether, for example, Confederation was a good idea. An Ontario student, 16 years old, can well be struck with that *thought*, and perhaps for the first time. "What did French Canada want out of Confederation?" Or a teacher who graduated in history may be teaching a class in English literature. Reading a poem from 1900, this teacher may find in it a reflection of the growing war fever and imperialism of the age. The 16-year-old student may *think* "So perhaps not all poems are supposed to be 'good'!"

A given school session is guided by a lesson plan, but in addition to the information the plan contains, there is the possibility that the lesson can be so presented as to awaken ideas in the minds of the students. Of course, students entertain ideas of all sorts, often private and irrelevant, in the course of the 40-minute lesson, but what interests me here are ideas that belong to the class material, even though not directly expressed, that can be awakened in the mind of one student or several of them. In a biology class, the student may be struck with the idea, and express the question, "So you mean that all mammals have the same organs?" In the case I have in mind, the thinking teacher will not say either "Of course they do!" or "No, they don't" so as to shut down discussion, but will understand the question and the reason for it, and will be able to guide the student into deeper areas of biology. In an interchange in class, the teacher will certainly have succeeded if the student now asks a further question, "But what about insects?" These are not merely the private ideas of the student; they were awakened by the lesson plan because they were a part of the material, a part of biology, even though not "taught," that is, not expressed. Such teaching is of course helped by the teacher's own grasp of biology, but even more by the teacher's grasp of *teaching*. One cannot teach without implementing some view (conscious or unconscious) about the ends of teaching—and the *thinking* teacher will certainly see the intellectual awakening of the student as one of the ends, in addition to transmitting information. The class will be conducted in such a way as to awaken ideas. Just as everyone can enjoy a joke, everyone can have an idea. The student is invited to think because the teacher does not merely think but fosters thinking through *acting out* thinking in the course of a class. Questions and remarks uttered *en passant* supplement the lesson plan.

The thinking teacher can take the initiative of setting up small research projects. In my junior high school, Tower Road School in Halifax, Nova Scotia, Mr. Gerald Mosher taught both English and French to our class. On one occasion he copied out for us a number of poems by Wordsworth, Coleridge, Shelley, Keats, and Byron (they were not in our text book), and, over a few sessions, he called attention to their differences of subject and style. Then he arranged an informal quiz: presenting us with further poems by these authors, but concealing their names, we were to see if we could tell who had written each one. I did well on the quiz: no doubt that helps me remember the occasion; but I also remember thinking, for the first time, that I might like some kind of literary vocation. This happened to me when I was12 years old, sixty years ago.

One particularly strong form of the teaching that thinks arises where the discussion moves closer and closer to what the teacher does *not* know. A timid teacher tends to avoid this territory, but some of the most memorable and valuable educational experiences arise when a teacher is led to say "I don't know." This can have the mild form, which is always memorable: "I'll have to look this up and tell you tomorrow," or it can take the drastic form, even more memorable: "Actually, Alice was right in what she said and I was wrong." One wonders why such occasions are not more common—teachers are hardly omniscient—and one reason, I suppose, is timidity. Even short of such occasions, though, a thinking teacher will always be mindful of the holes in his or her armor of knowledge, without being disabled by that recognition. This is an effect of the teacher's self-education: bumping up again and again against the border between what is known and what is unknown. It is not merely that self-education will expand the teacher's body of knowledge. Thinking is the activity in which we can discourse both about what we know and about what we do not know, that is, the activity of questioning.

Bildung and Truth

We can find a deep and moving account of *Bildung* in the address that J. G. Fichte delivered in 1811 when he was installed as Rector of the University of Berlin: "The One Possible Abridgment of Academic Freedom."[8] Though nothing was more important to him than academic freedom, his talk is taking aim at a corrupt form of it, namely, the insolent claims of student fraternities, composed usually of the nobility, who treated universities as their private fiefdoms where they strode about wearing special uniforms, armed with swords and pistols, provoking duels, drinking beer, and doing no academic work semester after semester. The University of Jena—where Fichte had had great successes and great defeats—was especially notorious for these fraternities, but it was not alone. Here Fichte is announcing that there would be no place for them at Berlin. In the fourth paragraph, he defines the vocation of the university in terms of *Bildung*: the faculty represents the generation that has received a *Bildung* through their predecessors, and the current generation represented by the students is to receive *Bildung* at the hands of the faculty, and there is plenty of emphasis on "solitude and freedom."

But this *Bildung* of one generation at the hands of another is linked by Fichte to a broader cosmological kind of *Bildung*. In the same paragraph, he introduces his own idealist doctrine that the visible world exists only to the end of making manifest the ultimate divine reality. It is principally in the excellences of the human race that the divinity becomes manifest, in the free actions of moral beings and in scientific truth, *Wissenschaft*. Free moral action exhibits the image of God, *das Bild des Göttlichen*. Since this action expresses our intelligence, our *Verstand*, it is preeminently in human *Verstand* that the divine image appears. Thus the *Bildung* of our intelligence is above all what lets God appear in the world. The continued forming of our intellect, *Fortbildung des Verstandes*, is most of all what fosters the divine work of world-forming, *Weltbildung*, and this is to be accomplished above all in the work of university *Bildung*. Therefore, Fichte's academic priesthood must free itself from all external worldly entanglements for concentration on its vocation.

Before proceeding, I shall look at some of the later fate, in Germany, of this ideal of *Bildung*, a sad, depressing history. It is evident that *Bildung* took on a bourgeois coloring during the nineteenth century that would make it repugnant to authors like Nietzsche and Heidegger. As with the English word "gentleman," it was the tone of snobbery that came to prevail, for *ein gebildeter Herr* was a German term that in the nineteenth century accomplished the same effect—marking a social distinction.

We need to confront the great fact of German history, that such tremendous ambitions as those of Herder, Fichte, Humboldt, Schleiermacher, and Hegel were to melt away through the course of the nineteenth century, to the point where they came to look ridiculous to succeeding generations. Universities and institutes and academies multiplied, and they grew in size, and new disciplines and specializations appeared, and when it began to seem that one could have a comfortable career as a scholar, the doubting and the indeterminacy and the openness of the older *Bildung* was often replaced by pedantry. Nietzsche, writing in the 1870s, noted that a typical German point of view was now to think that their *Bildung* and *Kultur* formed a point of national pride, marking them off from the French, for instance, and accounted for their victory in the war of 1871. These remarks appear in the essay of 1872 on David Strauss, the first of Nietzsche's *Untimely Meditations.* He sees this Strauss as a typical figure of the age. Once a theologian, Strauss had published a critical *Life of Jesus* in 1835 that scandalized the Establishment. But now, in his later life and separated from the church, Strauss came forward with a new humanistic-scientific religion of his own, presented under the title *The Old and the New Faith,* in which Nietzsche finds everything that he despises in the materialistic, mechanical, chauvinistic, imperialistic Germany of Bismarck's era. Strauss's book not only lacks both style and art (Nietzsche appends a devastating critique of Strauss's sentences and grammar), but it exhibits coarseness of feeling, self-satisfaction, and philosophical shallowness, enough to justify the title Philistine (this had always been the student's word for anti-intellectual lowbrows). But worse—Strauss was that particular kind of Philistine who specialized in the field of culture, who made a living by analyzing literature, art, philosophy, and religion. In Nietzsche's deadly phrase, Strauss was a *Bildungsphilister.* For Nietzsche, vulgar careerism, the mark of universities and so-called *Wissenschaft,* had swamped the arts and writing and genuine thinking. The intellects of old had been pursuers of the truth, not its possessors.

In some of Heidegger's writing of the 1930s we can see the same despair about *Bildung.* We have a lecture course from 1931–2 called *The Essence of Truth: On Plato's Cave Allegory and Theaetetus,* which aims to show that the *Republic,* in the Cave allegory, manifests a change in Plato's conception of truth.[9] (Originally Plato adhered to the ancient Greek tradition of *alētheia,* signifying Unconcealedness, but was led in his account of the Cave to a new conception, *orthotēs,* signifying Correctness, that paved the way for a great deal of later philosophy.) Since the education, *paideia,* of a philosopher is a conversion to truth, the treatment of truth must be expanded into an account of Platonic *paideia.* But Heidegger insists to his audience that this *paideia* must not be understood as *Bildung* (114). If we wonder why not, we are told that this incorporates a misunderstanding of Plato's Ideas, "made accessible for the superficiality of today: ideas as values, and *paideia* as culture and education [*Bildung und Erziehung*], i.e., what is most pernicious from the nineteenth century, but nothing from 'Antiquity' " (116). It is only the tone of rejection that we need note here, not the alternative reading of *paideia* and Ideas that Heidegger advances.

But the story of *Bildung* does not end there. It could be that if we confront and surmount the bourgeois deviation we shall find even deeper riches in the idea. We find, for instance, that Heidegger gave this matter further thought in the late 1930s and the 1940s, and his 1942 publication, "Plato's Doctrine of Truth" incorporated a more differentiated view of *Bildung*.[10] Here too he treats the allegory of the Cave, and Plato's changing conceptions of truth, and the link of truth to *paideia*, but now he is prepared to acknowledge the original idea of *Bildung* as in the period of German classicism, and to differentiate it from the bourgeois deviation, which he calls a "misinterpretation" (166). *Bildung* can be a rendering of *paideia* as long as we give proper heed to the *Bild* that constitutes its essence. We need to recognize a double character of *Bildung*: (a) the teacher is "forming someone in the sense of impressing on him a character that unfolds" (166). Here Heidegger has noticed the further "unfolding" of the *Bildung*, so that the impressing is not the stamping of the subject with an inert form but recognizes the subject's continuing active spirit. But then also (b): the formation proceeds "by antecedently taking measure in terms of some paradigmatic image, which for that reason is called the proto-type [*Vor-bild*]." *Bildung* is at once impressing a character on someone and being guided in that practice by a picture.[11] In the formation, *paideia*, that intervenes in the entire soul and being of the subject, what really counts is that prototype, *Vorbild*, whereby truth enters into the *paideia*, whereby it is not merely the massaging and processing of the subject, a mere insertion of information. The force of truth is the *Bild* of *Bildung*, whereas the mere forming of a subject into correct agreement with orthodox doctrine would not be a *Bildung* or a *paideia*. Might this conception too find application in practice?

In the greatest of all geometry lessons (Plato, *Meno* 82 b–85 b), Socrates leads a slave boy to recognize the *idea* of the diagonal of a square as a step to the construction of a double-sized square. This square with its diagonals is the *Vorbild* that is operative in the current lesson, shared by the two interlocutors. At a deeper level, there is the *thinking* that such a boy accomplishes in keeping with his rational soul, which is the *Vorbild* of humanity. There is a form of communication, whether through speech or through graphic displays, in which the positive information is seen to be surrounded by the hazy penumbra of what is questionable. The thinking teacher will know that this is more valuable than pure information, cut and dried. A tour of the solar system will certainly also have to touch down on Earth, and the mere representation of the celestial orbits can certainly be enhanced by the *thought*: "The Earth is rotating; we don't feel it." (A student may wonder, why, then, we do not feel it. Another may think we see it, in the cycle of night and day. This can lead to many enlightening vistas.) An intellectual awakening is not necessarily and not usually vocalized in questions, and education in general is largely an invisible and unverifiable process. But even as normal instruction is proceeding, the students get ideas. Whether we speak of "thinking" or of "ideas" does not matter, and for present purposes the two are very nearly the same thing. What I am calling "thinking" is an apprehension of something apparently true but which we do not understand and have the feeling of not understanding, something that is intriguing and puzzling, calling out for more attention, more inquiry. The student fortunate enough to have a thinking teacher will have confidence that this inquiry may succeed. Here I have been presenting an "idea" as the combination of a fact (the earth's rotation) with further unknown reaches (why we sense some things and not others), opening a road of inquiry that we would like to travel. Thinking may appear to be a process, and an idea to be an object of thought, but the two belong together. The ideas that matter in this context are not the private thoughts of the student, but something that is communicated by the lesson, even though perhaps not expressed by it. They are objective in that they belong to the discipline of instruction.

Intellectual awakening is just as valuable a part of education as the transmission of *doctrina*. The thinking teacher is communicating thinking to the students, a fulfillment of our common humanity of which every human being is capable. "Only those teachers who can freely question their own prejudgments, and who have the capacity to imagine the possible, can help students to develop the ability to judge and the confidence to think for themselves."[12]

Notes

[1] Martin Heidegger, *Sein und Zeit* (Tübingen: Niemeyer, 1927); translated by J. Stambaugh (Albany: SUNY Press, 1996). Page references are to the German text.

[2] Hans-Georg Gadamer, *Wahrheit und Methode* (Tübingen: Mohr Siebeck, 2nd ed. 1965); translated by J. Weinsheimer (New York: Crossroad, 1975). Page references are to the German text. See Jean Grondin, *Hans-Georg Gadamer: A Biography*, translated by J. Weinsheimer (New Haven: Yale University Press, 2003), 292–7.

[3] That is the argument of Gadamer's article, "The Universality of the Hermeneutical Problem," published in Gadamer, *Kleine Schriften I* (Tübingen: Mohr Siebeck, 1966); translated by D. Linge (Berkeley: University of California Press, 1976).

[4] *WM*, 7. See also Gadamer, "Herder und die geschichtliche Welt," *Gesammelte Werke* (*GW*), vol. 4 (1987), 318–35.

[5] Schiller's word was *Erziehung* rather than *Bildung*, but as Gadamer notes, this was of no consequence.

[6] Martin L. Manchester, *The Philosophical Foundations of Humboldt's Linguistic Doctrines:* vol. 32 of *Amsterdam Studies in the Theory and History of Linguistic Science* (Amsterdam: Benjamins Publishing Company, 1985), 161.

[7] "The Idea of the University: Yesterday, Today, Tomorrow," in Gadamer, *On Education, Poetry and History: Applied Hermeneutics,*" edited by D. Misgeld and G. Nicholson (Albany: SUNY Press, 1992), 47–59. Original in *Die Idee der Universität* (Berlin/ Heidelberg: Springer Press, 1988).

[8] *Über die einzig mögliche Störung der akademischen Freiheit,* published 1812; in *Fichtes Werke,* edited by I. H. Fichte (Berlin: Veit & Co., 1845–6), vol. VI, 449–64.

[9] *Vom Wesen der Wahrheit: zu Platons Höhlengleichnis und Theätet,* in Martin Heidegger, *Gesamtausgabe* (Frankfurt: Klosterman, 1988), vol. 34; translated by Ted Sadler (London: Continuum, 2002). Page references are to the German text.

[10] *Platons Lehre von der Wahrheit,* in *Geistige Überlieferung* (Berlin, 1942), separately in 1947, eventually in *Wegmarken* (Frankfurt: Klostermann, 1967). Translation by T. Sheehan in Heidegger, *Pathmarks,* ed. W. McNeill (Cambridge University Press, 1998), 155–82. In this case my page references will be to the *translation.*

[11] *"Bildung" ist Prägung zumal und Geleit durch ein Bild.* (166–7; translation altered.)

[12] Gadamer, "The Idea of the University," 58.

Chapter 5

Dialogue in the Classroom

Paul Fairfield

That the university classroom is the site not only of instruction but of intellectual investigation in one or another sense of the term is not a new idea. One finds traces of it already in Plato while in the modern literature it is a hypothesis especially associated with John Dewey, for whom education at all levels properly operates on a model of experimental inquiry.[1] A more recent trend prefers to speak of education as dialogical, in a sense that is reminiscent of but also distinct likewise from Platonic dialectic, Deweyan inquiry, and also hermeneutical dialogue as it would be spoken of by the foremost representative of post-Heideggerian hermeneutics, Hans-Georg Gadamer. The most noted proponent of dialogical education in recent decades is undoubtedly Paulo Freire, whose *Pedagogy of the Oppressed* and other writings interpret the concept of dialogue in an overtly political and Marxian vein. The movement of critical or liberation pedagogy that he inspired speaks of the educative process as an awakening to *conscientização* or critical reflection on the part of minds that have been systematically blinded by an ideology that conceals from them the truth of their condition at the bottom of the social order. The educator's role is to become a political militant of sorts and by means of emancipatory dialogue to pose questions and problems that reveal the truth about the students' condition. In Freire's words, "The struggle begins with men's recognition that they have been destroyed. Propaganda, management, manipulation, all arms of domination, cannot be the instruments of their rehumanization. The only effective instrument is a humanizing pedagogy in which the revolutionary leadership establishes a permanent relationship of dialogue with the oppressed. In a humanizing pedagogy the method ceases to be an instrument by which the teachers (in this instance, the revolutionary leadership) can manipulate the students (in this instance, the oppressed) because it expresses the consciousness of the students themselves." This passage captures the spirit and substance of dialogical education as this figure would describe it. Educators lead the students into non-authoritarian conversation about a given problem and take the dialogue in a critical direction without forcing them to adopt any particular beliefs. The direct inculcation of attitudes would constitute yet another "deposit" in students' minds, as the older "banking" concept had it, while "[a]uthentic liberation . . . is a praxis: the action and reflection of men and women upon their world in order to transform it."[2] The educative power of dialogue, for Freire, lies in its capacity to transform consciousness by raising it to critical awareness.

Dialogue as it is spoken of by Freire and the movement of critical education theorists resembles hermeneutical dialogue in some outward respects while retaining clear traces of objectivist epistemology. The educator remains the one who is in possession of critical knowledge while the students' consciousness is distorted by ideology. Given the Marxian problematic, dialogue is and is not hermeneutical, egalitarian, and reciprocal in about equal measure. This tension runs through much of the literature in this field, in spite of efforts to resolve it in a manner that Freire himself did not. The work of Nicholas Burbules is especially noteworthy in this respect. His important study, *Dialogue in Teaching*, endeavors to leave the legacy of positivism behind, but in a way that continues to owe rather more to Freire than to hermeneutics. As he expresses it, "Dialogue represents a continuous, developmental communicative interchange through which we stand to gain a fuller apprehension of the world, ourselves, and one another. In some cases, a dialogue might have an intended goal, such as answering a specific question or communicating an already-formulated insight. In other cases, however, none of the participants knows exactly where the dialogue is headed, or whether it will be successful; if one takes a process-oriented view of dialogue and its benefits, this uncertainty can be seen as educationally worthwhile."[3] Burbules' work undoubtedly represents an advance over Freire, particularly in replacing the latter's strident politicization of education with a more concrete description of dialogue as a practice of the classroom.

It remains, however, that this body of literature fails to draw adequately upon the resources of philosophical hermeneutics, a tradition rich in implications for education and nowhere more so than on the theme of dialogue in the classroom. Gadamer remains the foremost philosopher of dialogue of the past half-century, and his phenomenological descriptions of the practice have obvious relevance to what happens, or ought to happen, in the interaction between professors and students. My aim in this chapter is to speak of dialogical education in a more hermeneutical way than what Freire, Burbules, and others have done, drawing attention both to the conditions of the possibility of what properly goes under the name of dialogue and to several distorting influences that either undermine conversation in the university or in some cases hoist it with its own petard.

When Gadamer wrote of the art of conversation, he consistently emphasized the manner in which, phenomenologically speaking, the interlocutors are swept along in a process that they do not control. There is a certain receptivity and indeed passivity that characterizes our authentic participation in any dialogue that is worthy of the name. One of the most important passages on this topic from *Truth and Method* reads as follows: "We say that we 'conduct' a conversation, but the more genuine a conversation is, the less its conduct lies within the will of either partner. Thus a genuine conversation is never the one that we wanted to conduct. Rather, it is generally more correct to say that we fall into conversation, or even that we become involved in it. The way one word follows another, with the conversation taking its own twists and reaching its own conclusion, may well be conducted in some way, but the partners conversing are far less the leaders of it than the led. No one knows in advance what will 'come out' of a conversation. Understanding or its failure is like an event that happens to us. Thus we can say that something was a good conversation or that it was ill fated. All this shows that a conversation has a spirit of its own, and that the language in which it is conducted bears its own truth within it, i.e., that it allows something to 'emerge' which henceforth exists."[4] Gadamer was not speaking of education in this context, although the relevance of this description to our theme is clear. Classroom discussion as well "has a spirit of its own" and is "like an event that happens to us," one in which we are "less the leaders of it than the led," and so on. When it succeeds, education involves a voluntary relinquishing of control comparable to the at once active and passive nature of conversation, oriented as it is toward a critical examination of the subject matter and not a merely expertocratic bestowing of knowledge on docile minds. Insofar as anyone or anything presides over the conversation in an educational setting, it is the subject matter itself that does so, the text, problem, or question that orients the discussion, rather than any particular participant, be it professor or student.

Indeed, all of the conditions of hermeneutical dialogue of which Gadamer spoke have a direct application to the university classroom where the subject matter lies within any field of the human sciences. Good will, for instance, is indispensable to any classroom discussion and is a disposition that applies equally to the text and to the participants in the conversation. Inseparable from this is the anticipation that what our interlocutor has to say may be true and that our own point of view may be radically mistaken. Without the anticipation that the text that orients the discussion is saying what is true, or possibly true, and that the interpretations or judgments of a given student might be true as well, dialogue cannot succeed and in the usual course of things deteriorates into its opposite. Open-mindedness may well be the most essential condition of educational success in general; without it the mind is unteachable apart from the straightforward acquisition of information that merely confirms what one knows. This is not education in the preeminent sense of the word or possibly in any sense. Education makes demands upon us, and in the absence of a hospitality to ideas and the Socratic recognition of ignorance it cannot succeed, no matter how knowledgeable of the subject matter or how well versed in pedagogical technique the educator may be.

Dialogue requires as well a good deal of background knowledge, including a basic knowledge of the relevant field and its history. Were one teaching a course in political philosophy, for instance, and the students (or indeed the professor) lacked adequate knowledge of the major historical texts in this area, it is impossible that they could offer a contribution to the discussion that is both informed and moderately insightful. Their contribution in this circumstance will consist mostly in the repetition of elementary errors that a Locke or a Rousseau identified centuries ago. Regardless of the subject matter, one does not advance a conversation without knowing a good deal about its history. Nor does one advance it if one fails to read assigned texts or if the texts themselves are ill-chosen. If the professor unfortunately can do little about the former, they can nonetheless select texts that are important, relevant, and complete. In a discipline such as our own, for example, primary texts always have priority over secondary literature and textbook descriptions. From an informational standpoint, the most efficient means of learning the basic facts about the philosophy of a Plato or an Aristotle is undoubtedly the common practice of reading condensed and simplified accounts of the kind that are published every year in textbooks or, in even simpler form, on the internet. For many a student, and indeed professor, this quite suffices in preparing for multiple-choice and other antidialogical forms of examination, especially when the textbook description is supplemented with short excerpts from the primary texts. From a dialogical standpoint, this is comparable to having students of literature read plot summaries combined with a bit of thematic analysis. Students must be made to see that the great thinkers and texts of the past continue to speak to us; they are not antiques carefully preserved behind glass or objects to be gazed at or learned "about" without being engaged in the form of actually reading them in the old-fashioned way: slowly, carefully, and from cover to cover. Plato still speaks to us, but he no more does so via textbook summaries or short excerpts than Shakespeare does. The form of the Platonic dialogue, for instance, is no merely literary nicety or accidental garb that we can strip away in order to reveal the essential matter of the argument, one that we could formalize on a blackboard with a few numbered premises and a conclusion. Teaching Plato or any philosopher requires that we do justice to their texts, and this always means reading them first-hand and in their entirety. Only when the text is permitted to speak for itself does it become possible to offer a reply.

Formulating a reply also presupposes certain conditions of possibility, beginning with the well-formulated question. Conversation receives its basic orientation from a line of questioning, one that arises from the text or responds in a critical way to what emerges there. Most often it is the educator who introduces this, generally after having lectured for some period of time. Lecturing on the text or whatever subject matter is being discussed serves the dialogical purpose not of speaking in place of the text but of providing an interpretation of its major themes and clarification of some finer points as well as any relevant considerations that will help make the discussion an informed one. Lecturing is not an alternative to reading or thinking for oneself but is a means of ensuring that such thinking and discussion are based on an adequate understanding of the subject matter. Nothing is more hopeless than the classroom discussion in which students have not read the material and choose to rely on a professor's interpretation, or in which the conversation is premised on a basic misunderstanding of the text. In many disciplines it is now commonplace, for instance, for students and professors themselves to engage in vitriolic criticism of Freud without having paid him the courtesy of reading his work. It is a mystifying proposition that the issue of whether Freud was a sexist, or Marx a totalitarian, or Nietzsche a proto-Nazi, can be debated under this condition. It should give their educators pause when students have convictions about such matters that are based on information gleaned from a textbook.

Dialogue presupposes both informed participants and a common orientation toward a productive line of questioning. The art of leading discussion involves the difficult matter of keeping the question open while also moving the discussion forward. Conversation must not become stuck or go off the rails, but in what direction does it lead if we are to regard it as educationally productive? The answer will differ from Freire's; no matter what blinding prejudices we believe our students suffer from, educators are not revolutionists in the cause of emancipation, or not without falling into a kind of well-intentioned indoctrination. At the best of times they are experienced participants in the conversation into which they are initiating their students. It is a conversation that strives for a consensus that is seldom reached (and when it is reached, it is far from a guarantee of truth), for the articulation of new ideas, and ultimately for more conversation. The classroom discussion no more ends on a definitive note than does the conversation of philosophy itself. This is not a failure of inquiry but its usual condition, including when it is eminently rational. As Dewey would say, educative inquiry leads the students not to any final telos but to habits of mind that incline them toward further inquiry and to a love of ideas for their own sake. The point is to train students to join the conversation that is their culture, or some specialized discourse within it, and to cultivate the means of taking it further. Much of the point as well is to demonstrate the value of dialogue itself and to cast doubt on the notion that inquiry and education are mere means to an end, usually gaining a credential which itself is but a means. If understanding is indeed not only what we do but in a fundamental sense what we are, and if dialogue provides the wherewithal for understanding far more than any technique, then dialogue is a value unto itself which students in all fields of the human sciences must be made to see.

Among the more salient characteristics of dialogue as it occurs both within and without educational institutions is the lack of formal structure. Gadamer was correct to liken the structure of dialogue to that of play, with its repeated movement back and forth. What is to be noted about this play structure is its relative informality and fragility. Too much structure or control prevents a game from coming into its own and effectively removes the freedom of the players to invent novel moves, to use their judgment, form questions, and think outside the framework of rules laid out in advance. There is a haphazard quality in every genuine conversation. As the professor steps out of the role of the one who knows and assumes the role of interlocutor and Deweyan leader of inquiry, there is a relinquishing of control that allows the conversation to take on a life of its own and, in the usual course of things, to lead in a direction that no one anticipated. As the transition is made from lecturing to discussion, it behooves us, usually the professor, to pose a line of questioning and to invite students either to hazard a reply or to refine the question. If the appropriate conditions are in place, the conversation unfolds according to a dynamic of its own and all alike are swept along in a process over which no one altogether presides. If it falls to the educator to keep matters on the rails and prevent the conversation from deteriorating into the pedestrian and pointless, still the professor is neither authoritative judge, orchestral director, expert, nor preacher. The educative quality of such conversation consists precisely in articulating questions and judgments that others may challenge and in the testing of prejudices to which Gadamer referred. Often for the first time in a student's experience, opinions are formed and they are compelled to produce reasons for their views that others may challenge. They are taken out of the role of spectators and obliged either to account for their views or admit their inability to do so. Educative conversations generally remove our intellectual comfort by eliciting from us the semi-articulated judgments of which so much of our intellectual life consists. Real knowledge is never more than the tip of the iceberg of what we believe, gather, and suspect, and much as we may wish to limit our utterances to such knowledge, conversation has a way of drawing out of us the rest of the iceberg, sometimes at our peril and always in a haphazard way. The discussion is never quite the one that the professor anticipated, or when it is, it is likely due to overt or covert manipulation on the latter's part. The mind that refuses to relinquish control and to allow judgments to be made that conflict with one's own is unteachable, whether it be student or educator. If it falls to the latter to ensure that the conversation is properly informed, oriented by an intelligent line of questioning, and on the rails, it is not their role to ensure the conversation reaches a predetermined conclusion or indeed any conclusion.

A common tendency has us regard the unanswered question as a failure of inquiry. Classroom conversation seldom leads to a definitive conclusion or consensus; we simply run out of time, perhaps with a promissary note from the professor that we shall return to the issue next time. The professor knows, of course, that it will not be resolved next time either, and as the students head for the exit they will often sense that they have been shortchanged. This is an illusion, and demonstrating that it is one gets us to the heart of the matter of education, particularly in the human sciences. In principle, there is no last word in dialogue, no interpretation that is uniquely and supremely authoritative. Investigation comes to a definitive end only when the object is a problem that is strictly circumscribed in a technical discourse that sets out the terms of a possible solution. 2 + 2 = 4, and that is the end of the matter, even if we regard the rules of this discourse as conventions. In the human sciences one rarely places a QED beside one's judgments, or not without succumbing to the worst of intellectual vices. It belongs to the structure of conversation, as of wonder, to begin and end on a note of uncertainty and openness to further inquiry. The educative value of the conversation may lie in the question itself, posed from the student's point of view for the first time and which will lead one to read texts one otherwise would not have or to pursue the question in private reflection. What is urgent above all is that the student be taken out of the role of spectator, a role to which many are far too accustomed, and become an agent in their own intellectual life and in the conversation that is their culture. Educators need not and ought not concern themselves more than a little with the content of their students' beliefs but with whether they attain virtues of open-mindedness, inquisitiveness, and reasonableness that largely define intellectual agency.

If we would speak of what takes place in classrooms as dialogue, at least as a regulative idea, it is important that we bear in mind several conditions of contemporary education that seem rather to conspire against dialogue in any genuine sense of the word. When these conditions escape our notice, dialogue can become an empty catchword that begins to conceal more than it reveals about what actually takes place in classrooms. The lecture hall or seminar room is no ideal speech situation and indeed at times is not far from its antithesis. When this is so, a familiar cause is doctrinaire professors or equally doctrinaire students. The turn of mind that regards interpretations and judgments as incontrovertible certainties and that never tires of sharing these with one and all remains a phenomenon with which, I trust, we are all familiar. Students often appropriate not only their educators' views but, perhaps more important, certain of their intellectual dispositions, especially when these confirm dispositions of their own. The youthful mind that is inclined to be dogmatic has this disposition confirmed by educators who cannot abide having their positions challenged or who insinuate, subtly or unsubtly, that the students would do well to agree with the professor in classroom discussion or written work. Students are often acutely aware of an educator's level of tolerance for ideas with which they disagree or may know little about, and can emulate this attitude for better or for worse, quite aside from any substantive views that they hold. It is not uncommon in our own discipline, for instance, for students to gain the impression that mentioning the name of a philosopher to whom the professor is not well disposed is not a good idea. This is not unique to philosophy, and is equally common in fields with an overtly or covertly political content. Professors in such courses are not always receptive to critiques of whatever political stance they or a majority in their discipline uphold, as their students are often well aware. In an intellectual environment in which a great many ideas are deemed not only unjustified but "offensive," therefore off limits to discussion as a kind of point of order, dialogue consists in little more than ritualized utterances of the faithful. The most egregious example of this in recent decades is surely the political correctness phenomenon which has had a ruinous effect on universities everywhere it has found favor, but it is by no means the only one. The conversation in which the disposition toward the doctrinaire is given free reign is neither "inclusive" nor "empowering" but unintelligent and ill-fated.

Equally antithetical to conversation is the disposition that is the logical contrary of dogmatism and its dialogical equivalent. This is the subjectivism or relativism that is sometimes found among undergraduates. In this way of thinking, what is called "opinion-based" inquiry is to all intents and purposes arbitrary and is clearly distinguishable from what goes under the name of rational and verifiable investigation. When in the humanities the professor explains that the antithesis is false and that we are in a land beyond objectivism and relativism, the student can be at a complete loss as to how to proceed. The problems with the relativist's and the dogmatist's worldview are so many that one could not begin to enumerate them here, yet from an educative and hermeneutical standpoint their fundamental difficulty is that they likewise bring intelligent conversation to a halt. There is no reply to the proposition that x is true "for" someone or other, or that it is incontrovertibly true and there is no profit to be had in questioning it. The only rational reply, of course, is to question the statement's presuppositions, but such an inquiry is normally tangential to the discussion and therefore out of order. Either way, the conversation is at an end.

It comes to a halt as well when a spirit of apathy or ennui reigns, due to either poor instruction, failure to read assigned texts, a lack of background knowledge, or short attention spans. Other conditions that conspire against dialogue include an over-reliance on educational technology, such as the ubiquitous powerpoint presentation, with its darkened room and phantom professor. One does not carry on a conversation in the dark (or not one that is educative), when attention is fixed upon bits of information projected onto a screen, when one is unable to see the face of one's interlocutors and engage with them in some recognizably human way. Dialogue becomes a possibility when we put the technology away and when the professor stands and delivers a competent lecture before broaching discussion.

Conceptions of education that regard knowledge as so much useable information or on a model of what Jean-François Lyotard aptly termed performativity also run counter to the dialogical spirit of the university. When the business of education or the life of the mind generally is reduced to an affair of amassing information in the largest possible quantity, a view supported by a host of economic imperatives, we lose sight of the higher reaches of learning, particularly in the humanities. While no one will dispute that an education in history, for example, must include a good deal of information, it also involves cultivating a sense of history which surpasses the accumulation of facts. The nature of this sense and the business of instilling it are likewise ambiguous, yet where it is present it is most likely to have been cultivated in the back-and-forth of informed discussion. The same can be said of the student of philosophy or indeed any field of the human sciences. The educated student of philosophy possesses a sizeable knowledge of the great philosophical systems of the past and present, but when they lack the intellectual virtues and habits that make it possible to formulate questions and hazard interpretations of their own, capacities that again are cultivated in informal processes of discussion rather than in solitary reflection alone or in the accumulation of information, we shall not say that their education has been an unqualified success. Nor is an education in literature adequate until the capacities of interpretation and critique are cultivated in some appreciable degree, habits that again do not follow automatically upon acquiring information. The educated mind is generally characterized by intellectual dispositions that lead one to continue learning long after the period of formal education ceases, by a need to understand in a sense far broader than the mere stockpiling of memory.

Conditions that conspire against dialogue in the university classroom of today are many, and include an overly pragmatic view of education as a commodity or a credential, a narrow preoccupation with grades, a host of institutional inanities, and problematic personalities. The ethos of the classroom is of the highest importance to the matter of whether education succeeds or fails and is easily distorted through unintelligent emotionalism, clever sophistry, spotlight seeking, too few participants, too many students, and any number of other factors. Under the heading of institutional inanities I have in mind a good deal of what comes down to us from administrators and committees in the form of endless policies and rules which in most instances are either extraneous, irrelevant, or harmful. If the dialogical spirit is what we are endeavoring to cultivate, it falls to the students and the professor to bring this about, and apart from meddling there is little that nonparticipants in the conversation can do about this. What is called "an atmosphere conducive to learning" remains what Dewey spoke of as an ethos of experimental inquiry, one characterized by an uninhibited exchange of ideas in a spirit of good will or some semblance of it.

An important theme in Gadamer's hermeneutics is the limits of abstract methodology, and it is a theme of clear relevance to our topic as well. Notwithstanding the efforts of educational researchers to place this practice on the secure path of a science, there is no technique ascertainable by psychological or pedagogical science for promoting dialogue either within classrooms or without them. The stubborn fact for social scientists in this field (especially those still beholden to positivism) is that conversation is an art. It obeys no (or few) rules, is informal, and is a fragile achievement at the best of times. One can identify very general rules of thumb regarding how to "conduct" it, but here again we must recall Gadamer's remarks on the nature of this conduct: "the more genuine [also the more educative] a conversation is, the less its conduct lies within the will of either partner." This includes the professor, who is no master of ceremonies in the conversation but a participant or perhaps a coach of sorts. We can recall from our own student days those educators who possessed the seemingly magical ability to generate a high level of discussion through the sheer force of personality and passion for the subject matter while others struggled to elicit a single word from the students. What distinguished the former from the latter is no pedagogical technique but is more the nature of an intellectual disposition or set of these: enthusiasm, curiosity, open-mindedness, perhaps a sense of wonder or a bit of humor, but above all a conviction that ideas matter. These dispositions, as well as their opposites, are communicable to students, but not by means of a technique that can be spoken of in the abstract. Certain personalities take to the classroom like a duck to water while others will never feel at home there, no matter how much mastery of educational psychology or pedagogical science they acquire. Ideally, the professor imparts the conversational virtues by exhibiting them in his or her own person, and thus indirectly. Here Socrates remains our model: both the substance of the dialogue and the vital matter of its spirit are contingent on Socrates himself and the relentless search for the truth that he demonstrated and so imparted to his interlocutors while following no method but for the dialectic or the informal process of question and answer.

Much the same can be said of the art of lecturing. I have suggested above that lecturing on the subject matter is not an alternative to dialogue but an indispensable part of it. Were we to try to devise a technique of some tolerably precise kind for how to execute this task in such a way that we could guarantee that certain "learning outcomes" would be attained, we would be disappointed. Lecturing on the subject matter is clearly indispensable to university-level instruction, yet on the question of the method by which this is properly done the best answer remains the one proffered over a century ago by Dewey: "As to the question regarding the best method of lecturing, I can only say that I have been wrestling with the problem for some years, and have been regretfully forced to the conclusion that the best way a man can, is the best way for him to lecture."[5] This is about as helpful as we can be for the reason that we are speaking about a skill (or perhaps an art), which like other skills is acquired through habituation when it is acquired at all. Highly competent lecturers have little in common by way of technique and may follow no technique at all but adjust their approach depending on the complex factors surrounding a given course, the requirements of the subject matter, the background knowledge of the students, and so on. There is no one way of getting through to other minds, and any way that bears fruit is the best way. Nor is there a method of getting students to see what is important and what is trivial, what is questionable and what is less so. Lecturing is far superior to relying on textbooks for clarification, but apart from very general suggestions there is little by way of positive guidance and formalizable rules that can be devised. What it is essentially is a skill in presenting information or ideas in a fashion that is not only rigorous but that leads the students into engaging the inquiry in their own consciousness and in conversation. What lecturing is not, to cite Dewey once more, is a method of "pouring knowledge into a mental and moral hole which awaits filling."[6] Its aim, as with educational practices quite generally, is to contribute to the students' intellectual growth, and thus must be thought of more as a processual matter than the achievement of specific outcomes.

What ultimately drives the process is a need on the part of professors and students to understand what is true in a given field. Curiosity holds a certain authority here, and so as well does the ability to ask questions. This last matter refers not to the habit of getting a word in at every opportunity but to the skill of discerning what is questionable in a text or statement and formulating the question that brings matters into a state of illumination. As Gadamer well knew, "the path of all knowledge leads through the question. To ask a question means to bring into the open. The openness of what is in question consists in the fact that the answer is not settled. It must still be undetermined, awaiting a decisive answer." He knew as well that "[t]here is no such thing as a method of learning to ask questions, of learning to see what is questionable."[7] What propels the dialogue forward is precisely that which no method can teach. The logic of educative conversation remains the informal back-and-forth of question and answer, assertion and reply, in a process that searches for consensus and typically does not find it. When it does emerge, consensus is still no criterion of truth and as often as not indicates that conversation has merely reached a resting point or perhaps a dead end.

Dialogue as an educational ideal is rather more elusive and stringent than is often imagined, as is the case with the related hermeneutical theme of

Bildung. Conversation forms and transforms minds, and is not an optional extra that may be indulged in when the essential matter of transmitting information has been accomplished. Properly conducted, it leads students beyond the intellectual comfort of settled judgments and fortified systems of thought. Education in the preeminent sense requires that all of us subject our positions to the scrutiny of others, that we listen and learn, and that we criticize and question not only what the educator regards as obfuscating ideology but ideas of every kind, including the professor's. While dialogue is unlikely to revolutionize the society in quite the way that Freire imagined, it does belong to the higher reaches of university education.

Notes

[1] John Dewey's educational writings are numerous, but see especially *Democracy and Education* (1916), Middle Works Vol. 9, ed. Jo Ann Boydston (Carbondale: Southern Illinois University Press, 1980) and *Experience and Education* (1938), Later Works Vol. 13, ed. Jo Ann Boydston (Carbondale: Southern Illinois University Press, 1988).

[2] Paulo Freire, *Pedagogy of the Oppressed*, trans. M. Ramos (New York: Continuum, 2004), 68–9, 79. Also see *Teachers as Cultural Workers*, trans. D. Macedo, D. Koike, and A. Oliveira (Boulder: Westview, 1998); *Education for Critical Consciousness* (New York: Continuum, 1973); *Pedagogy of the Heart*, trans. D. Macedo and A. Oliveira (New York: Continuum, 2004); and Paulo Freire and Ira Shor, *A Pedagogy for Liberation* (South Hadley, MA: Bergin and Garvey, 1987).

[3] Nicholas Burbules, *Dialogue in Teaching: Theory and Practice* (New York: Teacher's College Press, 1993), 8–9.

[4] Hans-Georg Gadamer, *Truth and Method*, second revised edition, trans. J. Weinsheimer and D. G. Marshall (New York: Continuum, 1989), 383.

[5] Dewey, "Lectures vs. Recitations: A Symposium" (1891), Early Works Vol. 3, ed. Jo Ann Boydston (Carbondale: Southern Illinois University Press, 1975), 147.

[6] Dewey, *Democracy and Education*, 56.

[7] Gadamer, *Truth and Method*, 363, 365.

Chapter 6

On the Dire Necessity of the Useless: Philosophical and Rhetorical Thoughts on Hermeneutics and Education in the Humanities

Ramsey Eric Ramsey

Perhaps we ought to admit it so as to be more open to the surprises of dialogue: ideas we might be said to need are strange and come to us in ways, if we allow, befitting their weirdness. I had committed myself to this chapter's theme of making a defense of humanities education around the strange idea of the useless long before the latest round of attention would be bought to the issues surrounding education and the humanities: such attention as Patricia Cohen's piece in the February 24, 2009 edition of the *New York Times* on justifying the humanities in times of world-wide and national economic meltdown; by Mark Soulka's magnificent piece in *Harper's* detailing the loss of the humanities in the culture at large; as well as the journal *Polygraph*'s special issue on "Study, Students, Universities," a wide-ranging critique of the current state of affairs from a variety of critical perspectives.[1] Although times were difficult when I first decided to address this issue, these pieces and other news of the day tell us they are worse still. Indeed, the more pressing the economic crisis and the greater the desire for what many are calling "shovel-ready" thinking, the more outlandish the call for the necessity of fostering uselessness must seem. I am suggesting it is because of all these problems *more necessary to pursue the useless* as I shall attempt to show the useless is not the equivalent of the worthless. This strange idea should, I think, be with education all the time and in all times.

Even in "better times" I would find myself beginning with the following passage from Martin Heidegger. It comes from a lecture Heidegger gave, which we might consider a type of humanities seminar, as he was teaching students who had earned or were very near earning their medical degrees. Of their time (this was 1963) Heidegger says to them: "The most useful is the useless. But to experience the useless is the most difficult undertaking for contemporary man. Thereby, what is 'useful' is understood as what can be applied practically, as what serves an immediate technical purpose, as what produces some effect, and as that with which I can operate economically and productively. Yet one must look upon the useful as 'what makes someone whole,' that is, what makes the human being at home with himself."[2] Things have been bad for awhile. This passage, then, moves me to make my defense of uselessness in its terms, trying to defend humanities education and the dialogue fitting to it against its immediate takeover by the forces of utility, productivity, and technical purpose; this is an attempt to make good on what I think is the truth of this strange sounding passage.

I begin from these thoughts on education in the humanities around my work in the philosophy of communication and rhetoric and my commitment, long held, for the virtue of understanding philosophy as a way of life, a phrase made popular of late by Pierre Hadot. In an essay bearing this phrase as its title, Hadot begins to define philosophy as a way of life as a "mode of existing-in-the-world, which [has] to be practiced at each instant, and the goal of which [is] to transform the whole of an individual's life." Not the memorization of doctrines, philosophy undertaken in this manner understands "real wisdom does not merely cause us to know: it makes us 'be' in a different way."[3]

Another characteristic of philosophy as a way of life is its two-fold move of offering both a diagnostic and a therapeutic for troubled times. The stories that make sense of the difficulties contemporary persons suffer, those leaving us feeling homeless, are told by many voices; they include Heidegger's for whom the problem might be said to begin with Platonism, is intensified by Cartesianism, and made most dangerous by the hidden consequences of modern technology for thinking and language, and Nietzsche's for whom Platonism is also guilty but for differing reasons that lead to his understanding of Christianity's and scientism's culpability in all of this; and the voice of Marx who along with Engels understood in the nineteenth century that capitalism had already drowned in the "icy waters of egotistical calculation," then-held virtues of human being together, aspects of which we may still wish to rescue; and Adorno's for whom the total administration and instrumentalization of human being is—on his good days—dangerously close to being beyond redemption and on his bad days, well . . . worse. Yet all these stories also hold a utopian moment, even if each would not call it such.

As a result of these utopian echoes in the diagnostic stories I hear, I am able to hear other thinkers who offer therapeutics for the soul, such as to be eclectic and encourage transdisciplinary dialogue: Wilhelm Reich who helps us understand the transformative power of our own pleasures; and Oscar Wilde who makes socialism and art seem possible in ways Marx may have never imagined, or the filmmaker Marlene Gorris whose film *Antonia's Line* and the writer Marge Piercy whose novel *Woman on the Edge of Time* are two of the most utopian works one can imagine. Thinking from within this space of embracing philosophy as a way of life puts a necessary pressure on the boundaries, in the hope of weakening them, separating disciplines in the humanities. All disciplines in the humanities are able to teach the uselessness I shall be exploring here and to which Heidegger's words have pointed me. It is a hermeneutic lesson that rightfully broadens philosophy to acknowledge many texts and types of texts become for us chances to think philosophy as a way of life, to think about how we might "be" in a different way.

The body of this chapter is in three sections. I begin with some brief words on philosophy and rhetoric to show that hermeneutics is at the heart of being human and thus education in the humanities. This will be the backdrop for my interpretation of Plato's famous cave allegory from the *Republic* focusing on those moments where talk is essential to the pedagogical proceedings and where I shall disclose my understanding of the useless. This reading of the cave allegory, which also, I believe, provides evidence of the originary nature of hermeneutics, will offer us some insights with which in the brief final section to defend the virtue of fostering the useless in humanities education.

Hermeneutics at the Heart of Being Human

In his wonderful essay "Rhetoric Resituated at the End of Philosophy," Calvin Schrag helps us understand why the future study of philosophy will be inextricably linked with the study of rhetoric and communication when the abstract and narrowly defined epistemological understanding of philosophy comes to an end.[4] By way of what he calls a posture of hermeneutical and rhetorical recovery and retrieval, we are shown in this essay an interpretation of both philosophy and rhetoric so we might think with them anew. A keener understanding of both concepts is provided when they are brought back from philosophical abstraction to the lifeworld of rhetoric's original concern, back to talk and communication, back to a thinking and conversing with one other in such a way that philosophy and our communicative being-in-the-world cannot be separated. When we understand philosophy as hermeneutics and rhetoric as social interconnectedness, we see interpretation and communication as part of the inescapable structure of the human condition and not merely techniques we sometimes employ when we either wish to know something or when we wish to send a message to a receiver.

Rather than abstracting from the lifeworld of our everyday being together, we begin from within our social relatedness. In beginning here we face the challenges of thinking about understanding from within understanding and thinking about communication from within communication.[5] Ultimately, we could say there is no place that stands outside of understanding or outside communication whence we could see either without already being involved in both. This is neither a vicious circle nor one to be simply tolerated; it is the space from within which we must find what Heidegger calls the "most primordial possibility" of understanding. Being who we are—finite human beings—is to have to begin from within this circle. Such an understanding of our finitude, Schrag writes, "renders explicit the common space in which the philosopher and the rhetorician move about," and what is shown to us then is not a narrow epistemological starting place of subjects and objects but rather "the broader more vibrant hermeneutical space of affect-imbued and praxis-oriented engagements."[6] Following upon these insights we are able to turn Aristotle's claim in the *Rhetoric* concerning *logos*, *ethos*, and *pathos*, so fundamental to that book's themes, in another direction away from the derivative textbook-version of Aristotle where *logos* is said to be reason, *ethos* is said to be character, and *pathos* is said to be emotion with respect to publicly delivered discourse.

In the wake of rhetoric resituated at the end of philosophy and by taking the hermeneutical circle as constitutive of our being-together, we can understand *logos* by another term found in the *Rhetoric*: *phronesis*. Taking off from Gadamer's reading of Book Two of the *Rhetoric* and Book Six of Aristotle's *Ethics*, we understand *phronesis* as the beginning of all our thinking and not simply in its traditional way as prudence or practical wisdom.[7] *Phronesis* so conceived announces the understanding we always already are within the inescapable circle of interpretation. To hold as we do that hermeneutics is at the heart of being human is now to say *phronesis* is the *logos* at the heart of our being-in-the-world as always already understanding something. From within the hermeneutical circle so understood, *ethos* is envisioned as a way of saying human being is always a dwelling; it describes our embodied being-in-the-world and our lived embodiment of world and words, not simply our character. *Ethos* here, as it is for others thinking in this vein, is linked to ethics and thus linked to communication and its essential place in negotiating social relationships. Finally, to move *pathos* from being reduced to its textbook version, we see it no longer simply as an abstracted sense of emotion but as a way to say we are always having to suffer others and otherness. We are always in the face of something other than ourselves, and having to undergo this otherness is always moving us in some manner or another.

If we thus understand the hermeneutical circle as consisting of these three concepts, then one way of orienting education is to attempt to address our thinking to the interplay among each in our humanities seminars. In a way only to be alluded to here, I assign three ways of approaching the thinking of *phronesis, ethos,* and *pathos,* one more or less, although clearly not exclusively, to each: hermeneutics as the study of *phronesis,* the always already understanding of our worldliness; rhetoric as the study of *ethos,* the always embodied dwelling in words; and theology as the study of *pathos,* the inescapable otherness of our being-in-the-world. Rhetoric awaits at the end of philosophy because it had been there from the beginning, but hermeneutics and theology were there as well. Heidegger writes of the concept being-in what he could well have written also about *phronesis, ethos, pathos,* as I understand them: "[it] is not a 'property' which Dasein sometimes has and sometimes does not have, and without which it could be just as well as it could with it. It is not that man 'is' and then has, by way of an extra . . ." these qualities.[8] Thereby these three concepts always appearing together in human being-in-the-world are also not something added on to a subject that could be said to exist without already being made up by them.

Against the backdrop of intertwining hermeneutics and rhetoric (and guided by insights from Heidegger in his brilliant *The Essence of Truth*), we shall focus interpretive attention at two moments in the cave allegory where human beings talking with one another plays a central, if often overlooked, role in the story.[9] This telling of this famous story is, I have little doubt, a version objectionable to Platonists of the letter but, I am hopeful, will have a ring to it in the ears of those pedagogues who understand themselves as the spiritual heirs of Socrates. Consequently, we shall try not for a Platonic way out of the cave, not an epistemological escape where each step turns us to objects that are merely more real, but in keeping near the claim that hermeneutics is at the heart of being human, we seek another way out or at least another way of understanding what the task and challenge of our education shall entail.

Listening to Talk in the Cave Allegory

Despite asking to go back again to a classic text, I do so understanding fully well there will not be a suitable premodern solution to our so-called postmodern problem. Going back to philosophy, rhetoric, and theology will, of course, require nuance and careful thinking because we cannot act as if we could have gotten back to anything without having come from where we find ourselves today. Our historically embodied existence is not like that. We can only get back by passing through the hermeneutical and rhetorical habits standing between now and then and, conversely, any then can only appear to us now by way of the same historical passages and pathways.

That said, let us approach this interpretation of the cave allegory beginning at line 514a of *The Republic* where we are told by Socrates the whole of the allegory is a ". . . situation which you can use as an analogy for the human condition—for our education or lack of it." From the very beginning of the story we are being asked to be attuned to education. This contextualizing move that focuses on education, which provides the hermeneutical hint I embrace, is then followed by the famous description of the prisoners' initial condition. This situation is the situation out of which and from within which education, if it can, will have to happen if we follow Socrates' opening words. Of course, we will recall the story places them chained such that they are forced by the conditions of their imprisonment to be able only to look forward to the cave's back wall. We are told further about the goings on behind them, of how shadows are produced by persons carrying artifacts above the conjuror's wall and in front of the fire casting off its light; and we are told how these shadows thus appear on the back wall of the cave. So positioned, facing the back wall, the prisoners find themselves watching shadows pass before them.

"A strange picture you are painting with strange inhabitants," Glaucon tells Socrates after hearing this description, and even we who have learned to grant fantastic stories their conceits might agree with him. Yet Socrates in the next line seems to want to make things stranger still. In response, Socrates' provocation is this: "They are no different from us." Before we can read on a question arises within us: These pitiful prisoners are no different than we are? So we are told. It now seems we shall have to listen with an altogether different orientation as now we are the strange inhabitants of this circumstance. One line of text has the profound effect of moving us from mere onlookers and passive listeners to this strange story to becoming its protagonists. We have been moved such that we are now implicated in every word of the story. Socrates is good at this, not just getting to the heart of the matter but of getting *your* heart, *your* psyche at the center of the dialogue. Of all we might say in praise of him what I wish to emphasize here is this: Socrates is as great a rhetor as he is a philosopher. Moreover, he understands there is no discernible distance between the two. He seems here to understand the lesson outlined above: philosophy and rhetoric are always intertwined.

Here we are in the middle of things. This is not an easy place to occupy in this story. It is uncomfortable being situated such. There may be a lesson here that we unwittingly resist. When interrogating the cave allegory we cannot slip easily into the belief that Socrates tells of some situation other than our own. We need to be reminded: we are they—when it comes to the prisoners and their condition *we are in this trouble with them.*

For all this trouble we are in, a hope comes to us in the next lines of the allegory and it comes because of communication. In what seems to be a line easily overlooked, Socrates at this point says: "Now, suppose they were able to talk with one another. . . ." In this supposition a key to thinking philosophically and rhetorically about education is disclosed to us. We can talk with one another—how miraculous. That wonder aside for the time being—and a type of theology might be waiting for us when we return—let us focus on the topic of such talk. What we talk about, we are told by the text, is what is at hand, what is there before us on the wall, and before us every day and all the time. Would not our words be understood as being in and about the *only* world disclosed to us, the world of shadows? We talk of shadows but not of nothing. Because of this sharing in speech the shadow condition is real and meaningful. Let us put it this way: when these talking prisoners talk they talk of what is disclosed to them, they talk about what they are able, about what is given to them in their condition. Indeed, their talk would be of shadows, and yet I find this moment filled with undischarged utopian potential, to paraphrase a thought of Ernst Bloch. We remain prisoners, it is true, because our conversations more often than not confirm and solidify our enchained condition. We can put a finer point on it by saying if as prisoners we only talk to other prisoners about a shadow-imprisoned world, then we would believe the whole of the world to be exhausted by this discursive understanding.

Nevertheless, the ability to talk with one another about what shows itself to us is never at a remove from our hermeneutical condition, and this is Utopian because talking about what shows itself is also what will act as the condition for the possibility of our becoming freer, which in the allegory means becoming better educated about who we are and what we share.

The hope of education is seeing that the prisoners are not without sight altogether or in a meaningless place, just in a place poorly lit. The moment that matters here is that the endowment that we are as the opening to even this dim firelight is an opening equiprimordially constituted by showing and speech.

The prisoners, to use a Heideggerian phrase, "live in the truth" and as truth-dwellers are always sharing a world, sharing a reality, sharing the meaningfulness of being together. Following Heidegger, I am focusing attention here not toward what we see, not toward the content of what shows itself, here still shadows, but toward how we are the condition for the possibility of anything showing itself at all. If this could be put straightforwardly, we would say, even as prisoners, we are already living in the truth, living in the disclosure of world and sharing meaning. The truth of the hermeneutical circle is exemplified here. We do not have to invent ways, primordially at least, of how to get our words about the world to the others; we speak and they understand something because the light already is and we in it. Hereupon it becomes apparent no matter where we begin we are always already the seeing of the light.

Thereby, already in the depth of the cave talking about shadows, we have learned a fundamental lesson about ourselves. Yet we have more to learn. As the allegory continues to unfold this shared world of shadows in the least lit part of the cave is subsequently shattered for one of the prisoners when she is released from her shackles. She is reoriented by someone or something—"set free," as Socrates puts it. This freeing turns her around to face the conjurer's wall, the artifacts that appear above it, and the fire itself. Following the hint with which we began, this turning, or reorientation, this setting free is the analogy for education.

There is a problem, however. The beginning lesson of our education is not well received; indeed, the allegory uses the following words to describe our reaction to our new orientation: "dazzled," "hurt," "pained," "bewildered," "overwhelmed." Our first move in freedom increased, our response to education is to turn away, to go back, to return to the familiar. The freed prisoner desires to return to her chains. Let us understand this resistance to our education hermeneutically and rhetorically. We re-turn to familiar hermeneutical ways of seeing and interpreting the world by going back as quickly as possible to those vocabularies and those words that feel comfortable, whose habituated comfort lessens the bewilderment, soothes the pain, and takes us from an overwhelmed state back to a kind of security in the face of hearing and seeing what is otherwise than that to which we had grown accustomed.

However, on the reading to which I am testifying here, the dazzle caused by our turning toward the firelight is not from seeing that the artifact of let us say a cat (which we now see) is more real than its shadow which we had been seeing. At the core, the dazzle is from the firelight itself and from learning that human being is the "site" where the light shows. We are dazzled by coming to understand what we make possible by being the *there* where light is allowed and by the never-ending responsibility this will entail. Clearly, the allegory teaches that being dazzled follows upon not having our backs turned any longer. Yet as prisoners, from what had we been turned away in the first place? We had been turned away from a hermeneutical and rhetorical understanding of ourselves.

In this first turning we gain confidence for the reading offered above about our place in the hermeneutical circle. It is here one learns what education has left to accomplish because suffering the light is both as necessary for one as one is unprepared for it. We must find ways to resist the initial desire to forfeit our freedom and remain facing ourselves and the tasks this sets out for us. Endowed as openness to the light as the condition of being human yet unconditioned for taking this all in without practice is the human condition calling for education.

This powerful lesson is the first but not the last we shall need, and more awaits us in the next stage of the story. Our educated escapee now graduates to a place completely outside the cave where she experiences a similar bewilderment in the light of the sun as she did in the first turning from facing the cave's back wall to facing the firelight. Yet this time I imagine her more patient with what befalls her there and with good reason. She has been prepared by the education of her first turning inside the cave to suffer with the requisite persistence this new realm of the sun-lit place outside the cave. Here she further clarifies the understanding she is gaining of her place in discourse and disclosure. To turn the obvious phrase: she understands what her place in the sun makes possible. In keeping with the reading offered here, I want to suggest her feeling at this stage as well comes not from an epistemological realization outside the cave—exemplified by the phrase: "oh, there's a real cat, I get it now"—but from a hermeneutical–theological realization. If the famous dictum to "know thyself" now means understanding one's place in discourse and disclosure, then she is coming to understand herself as the intertwined moments of *phronesis*, *ethos*, and *pathos*.

At this point with her ascent complete she has been exposed to everything we might call the geography of the tale has to offer. Although one might think the story could end here, leaving our escapee educated and basking in the sun, it, of course, does not. Neither she nor we with her have yet to be exposed to other essential lessons the allegory has left to teach. To follow the allegory further allows us to see the tasks set for education in the humanities, and why I believe it will require the study of hermeneutics, rhetoric, and theology.

As hermeneutically and rhetorically implicated beings, our given condition remains a shared condition with others, even after reorientation and an ascent into the light of the sun. Remembering whence we came and those who were there with us in the world we shared before belongs to this new understanding. Thus, Socrates says, the one who stands outside the cave is able to recall how it used to be, is able to recall what she used to think and believe, and thus she is able to recall in a sympathetic way what those still in her former world are likely thinking, saying, and suffering.

This compassion, Socrates suggests, means one who has entered the most lit place outside the cave and who tries to understand her fundamental relation to light and openness feels happy about her altered circumstance and sorry for those she left behind. In a scene from the cave allegory that follows upon the accomplishment of this coming to self-understanding and where talk is again essential, we meet a version of the notion of uselessness that motivates these thoughts and provides the provocation of its title. Uselessness shows itself with respect to the escaped one's return after her experience of reorientation to the once-shared world she left behind. It is important to remember she returns to a *world*, one that is real because it is being shared in the prisoners' talk. Furthermore, the sharing of a world occurs because it has embedded in it ways of interpretation and practices of evaluation determining what will count as success in the world being shared. By habit we tend to naturalize our worlds and take their givenness for granted. That is until someone says something otherwise.

This is what is imagined in the allegory at that place where we now linger. The one who returns tries to talk of what she has learned, tries rhetorically to share her self-understanding. We imagine she recommends such an understanding in her conversation with those with whom she speaks in her old world. I would say she tries her hand at teaching the virtue of reorientation. "It is better for all of us if each of us understands who we are and what we have in common," she might be heard to say. Such speech, however, will not be well received, Socrates tells us. What she has to say sounds out of this world to the prisoners' ears. From our hermeneutical and rhetorical standpoint we understand why. Her talk sets her at odds with her fellows so much so that Plato seems to offer us this rhetorical situation as a way of reminding us of the outcome of Socrates' public self-defense of philosophy as a way of life as recorded in the *Apology*.

"If your understanding is so wonderful and accomplished, then you can prove it," the prisoners demand. This will be a problem, to say the least, because what counts as proving in the prisoners' lifeworld has well defined rules that are not open to debate. Putting it another way, she is forced to prove her case in a practice already determined and will be evaluated by its rules, by how words work in that world. In the terms of this reading, the prisoners ask her to prove the usefulness of her education. Accordingly, she is forced to contest for honors and prizes in their world in a game of who can identify shadows the fastest and most precisely.

No reader of the allegory needs reminding, she loses the contest. Of course she loses, how not? As Gadamer might say, she could never prove this as one cannot prove one's self-understanding, she can only be answerable for it; she is trying to say how human beings are not what objects are. As a result, caught in the context of proof and by the values of the contest, her education is judged useless and she along with it. Such uselessness so judged is not welcomed in this world; indeed, if the prisoners could break free they would take her life, Socrates speculates. Having been reoriented she seems to the prisoners "all turned around" as the colloquial phrase would have it. As the loser of the contest we infer from the text she will receive no awards or honors; she will be granted no power nor will any laudatory status be given to her.

Yet following the passage from Heidegger with which this chapter began, I cannot help but think the reorientation—the education—we try taking away from the allegory, despite its obvious dangers, is to cultivate in our education her uselessness for ourselves. I am suggesting uselessness is the preferred condition to be developed, cultivated, and fostered in light of the lessons of the cave allegory read this way. The prisoners' usefulness and success in the shadow game is real and consequential to be sure; worse still it rules, and harshly at that, vast stretches of the world. Even if we grant usefulness its overwhelming reach, and who could deny it, we misunderstand its limited value if we mistake the *vital* lesson of the allegory to be simply knowing that shadow cats are less real than artifact cats which are less real than real cats. The hermeneutical lesson is rather, I am confident, to see our place in discourse and disclosure and to find words and ways to say how seeing and sharing in communication is possible. To desire uselessness on my reading of the cave allegory is to prefer this search for ourselves over our mere utility.

What remains true from first to last in the allegory is this: we share and confirm our place in the world through communication. This returns us, the tradition is trying to tell us, to *phronesis*, *ethos*, and *pathos*. Brought back to hermeneutics, rhetoric, and theology we stand at this moment in dire need of inventing ways of thinking, talking, and being-together to confront rhetorical situations as urgent as the one our educated prisoner faces upon her return to the cave. We need to find speech that can be persuasive about the most pressing of matters that cannot be proven, while acknowledging we must do so under less than ideal conditions. How can we help the reoriented one be understood? What shall we say, to what rhetorics and stories shall we turn, what ways shall we have to invent, to share, and to be answerable for what she understands about being useless? How shall we make ourselves capable of listening to her tale? As we know from our own experience, education deals with such questions by carrying out in conversation, in writing, and in performance embodied responses to these pressing questions.

As an inexhaustible and tireless text, the cave allegory is never finished. However, to summarize for the task at hand I would say: A funny thing happened on the way to the truth; we thought when we got to the bottom of things all would be well. From some imagined certain foundational truth we dreamt of being told by some method or blueprint exactly what to do and how to do it. The bottom of things encountered at the end of philosophy, however, turned out to hold a surprise for us. From among the many we might have chosen, I share an example of this turn-around from Gianni Vattimo's fine book *Belief*: Whereas G-d as the word made flesh had for so long in theology come to save us from the fears of our inexactitude and our finitude, G-d as the incarnation of the word today has the task of assuring us of our provisional character, assuring us of the necessity of friendship and conversation for our relative and historical nature, and assuring us we are never finished, neither with ourselves nor with our responsibility to others.[10]

To illuminate this further, what Schrag, Vattimo, and Jacques Derrida, for instance, show us is the need for this type of theological thinking.[11] Not only in helping us understand how we can try to meet the responsibility of suffering our being-together, but also showing us how such talk comes in this historical moment to offer the words necessary to such an understanding. I can only list here what some of those words might be which we could put to work: sharing, indebtedness, and gratitude; testimony, gift, and love; maybe those can get us started. But getting started means always remaining underway. Living in the truth experienced at the bottom of things and encountered in the allegory announces a calling to responsibility, to having to undertake living as an inexact endeavor, a calling to embrace ourselves as beings who are never finished yet always answerable in communication for as far as we have gotten together.

Seeking Good Company

It is an allegory, after all. We are not, as they say, "literally" in a cave. Nonetheless, we are in a world and in words, in contests that have evaluative presuppositions all of which seem to be embedded so deep as to appear unchangeable. Utility and marketability are two such rules of the game as it is currently being played. Both can take their toll on education understood in the hermeneutical light of the allegory. Nonetheless, here is some good news for education announced in the reading of the allegory offered above. We are neither required nor able to give students or ourselves the original endowment of *phronesis, pathos, ethos.* That is to say, we are, by being who we are, already readied for education. Our task is related to this endowment of readiness for education in a two-fold way that pushes against disciplinary boundaries and seeks to open us to the experience of the uselessness Heidegger advocates. Our task shall be trying from as many disciplinary perspectives as possible to disclose the structures that make up our shared being-in-the-world, so to see hermeneutics at the heart of being human as well as experimenting and imagining how we might go about making something other—something happier as Aristotle might be made to say—within our historically embodied endowment.

By design, colleges and universities place people in good company, into a community already undertaking the hard work of understanding what it will take to be at home with oneself. In her essay on culture and freedom Hannah Arendt writes that if we inhabit this community well, "then we shall know how to reply to those who so frequently tell us that Plato or some other great author of the past has been superseded; we shall be able to understand that even if all criticism of Plato is right, Plato may still be better company than his critics . . . then we can be what a cultivated person ought to be: one who knows how to choose his company among men, among things, among thoughts, in the present as well as the past."[12] While calls for technological success, shovel-ready practical application, and profitable exchange abound, universities in general and humanities programs in particular are places, one of the few left in the modern world, where space and time are set aside for the slow and careful craft of thinking and dialogue.

How miraculous that still today in an age demanding all this there are such places and such times. We already know from all the hard work we do daily, safeguarding such time and space is not easy. We know for instance how difficult it is to explain why the rhythm of university life should not always try to meet the rhythm of the larger culture of which it is a part, even if it must always be in conversation with it.

To embody our commitment to the worthiness of the slow and carefully cultivated in education, let us suppose, following upon the cave allegory, that we can talk with one another and that there are better and worse circumstances in which this dialogue can occur. We already do this by assigning those texts allowing us to talk about interpretation, talk about words, and talk about otherness and transcendence from our varying perspectives. Year after year a new class of students who embody a readiness for education arrive to places and practices set aside for them. We try to show them this loving struggle, as Jaspers calls it, has been ongoing for centuries in the words and deeds of our predecessors. In the course of joining and continuing such useless conversations and sojourning toward home from within our homelessness, we attempt to make a fitting place for coming together, make way for the surprises conversation often engenders, and we learn how to make way for otherness.

A word more about Socrates. Hadot is fond of reminding us Socrates is *atopos*, atypical, uncommon, disruptive; "Socrates is *weird*," in Martha Nussbaum's words. As Alcibiades notes in *Symposium*, the stories Socrates tells seem so simple, almost dull and self-evident until we think about them not from the outside looking in but from the inside looking in, taking them to heart—somehow—within the lives we are trying to live. "But isn't it, in the end, just a story and an old one at that," the utility- and market-minded are apt to ask. I think, as Paul Tillich taught me to say in another context, we respond in this one by saying: "No, no it's not just a story, it's nothing less than a story." With his talk and stories and the philosophical life we are told he lived with others, Socrates sought to bring it about that others also became *atopos* with respect to the normal way things were going on around them. This madman even had the audacity to ask that others be grateful for the disruptions his dialogues caused them. In the face of everything, Socrates never let up in his reorienting endeavors. And neither shall we.

To close, then, with a few questions to keep a dialogue going: can we learn to welcome the wonder of this weirdness as our advantage? Can we welcome our inexactitude and remain answerable to it by thinking about it with care, spontaneity, and rigor? At last, can we welcome the idea of and be thankful for an education that makes us, in a word, Useless? We are able to do all of these things. To be sure, the allegory tells us it is our essence to be so able. Whether we shall indeed express our gratitude along these lines remains a question to be answered every day by undertaking the genuine task of education.

Notes

1 Patricia Cohen, "In Tough Times, the Humanities Must Justify Their Worth," *New York Times,* February 24, 2009; Mark Souluka, "Dehumanized," *Harper's* September 2009, 32–40; *Polygraph: An International Journal of Culture and* Politics, 21 (2010), "Study, Students, Universities," eds. Luka Arsenjuk and Michelle Koerner, 1–13.

2 Martin Heidegger, *Zollikon Seminars: Protocols–Conversations–Letters,* ed. Medard Boss, trans. Franz Amyr and Richard Askay (Evanston: Northwestern University Press, 2001), 159–60.

3 Pierre Hadot, *Philosophy as a Way of Life,* ed. and trans. Arnold I. Davidson (Oxford, UK: Blackwell, 1995), 265.

4 Calvin O. Schrag, "Rhetoric Resituated at the End of Philosophy," *Quarterly Journal of Speech* 71 (1985), 164–74.

5 This is worked out in another register in Ramsey Eric Ramsey, "Nothing Outside of Circumstance," in *Perspectives on Philosophy and Communication,* edited by Pat Arneson, (West Lafayette: Purdue University Press, 2007).

6 Schrag, "Resituated," 171.

7 Hans-Georg Gadamer, *Truth and Method,* trans. Joel Weinsherheimer and Donald G. Marshall (New York: Continuum 1989), see especially 310–21.

8 Martin Heidegger, *Being and Time,* trans. John Macquarie and Edward Robinson (New York: Harper and Row, 1962), 84.

9 Heidegger, *The Essence of Truth,* trans. Ted Sadler (New York: Continuum, 2002).

10 Gianni Vattimo, *Belief,* trans. Luca D'Isanto and David Webb (Palo Alto: Stanford University Press, 1999).

11 From among the many relevant works here, these: Calvin O. Schrag, *God as Otherwise than Being* (Evanston: Northwestern University Press, 2002); Jacques Derrida, *Specters of Marx: The State of the Debt, the Work of Mourning, and the New International,* trans. Peggy Kamuf (New York: Routledge, 1994) and *Acts of Religion,* ed. Gil Anidjar (New York: Routledge, 2002); and Gianni Vattimo, *After Christianity,* trans. Luca D'Isanto (New York: Columbia University Press, 2002).

12 Hannah Arendt, *Between Past and Future* (New York: Penguin, 1954), 225–6.

Chapter 7

Hermeneutic Education to Understanding: Self-Education and the Willingness to Risk Failure

Andrzej Wiercinski

In the traditional understanding, *educare* means to lead the pupil from a state of ignorance to certain wisdom. It describes the process of bringing up, rearing, training, the dynamics of drawing knowledge out of somebody, or leading one out of ordinary thinking. Learning must be understood as proceeding via dialogue, which is the essence of education as the practice for exercising freedom. The Greek word *paideia* connects learning with *ethos*, the habit of living the good life.[1] *Paidagogos* means a tutor and guardian of boys, a leader or custodian who is responsible for a child. Since a *paidagogos* leads the pupil toward maturity, we can say that it is leading one toward love, as in the final line of Dante's "La Divina Commedia," "The Love which moves the sun and the other stars."

The philosophical *paideia* of Socrates is concerned with self-awareness through thinking, becoming awakened and strengthened through argumentation. The realization of philosophical potential happens in the Socratic conversation with its main task of assisting people in avoiding "being talked out of the fact that there is such a thing as the Just, the Beautiful, and the Good."[2] The hermeneutic virtues of education cannot be acquired by the study of education and tested by academic experts, but are active conditions for deliberation, choice, and action. To educate a human being is not to teach someone a trade or an art, but to cultivate sensitivity toward exercising one's freedom. Education is not about an accumulation of information, in the sense of producing measurable outcomes, or an increase in experience. Primarily it is about the will to learn about oneself while dealing with others. It is about learning from them, learning to understand and to share the concerns of the other. Education is never ethically neutral. It is always concerned with providing a human being with ethical intelligence and is a process leading toward ethical responsibility. It is about facing the face of the other and recognizing the ethical responsibilities of a *paidagogos* and a student toward each other. The phenomenon of education is the paradigm for human interpretative experience.[3]

Education cannot be reduced to so many answers to the demands of individuals and of the society. It is less about duty than engagement. By engaging the whole person we are getting acquainted with him or her and experiencing the person from their basic conviction. This kind of existential opening toward the other results in a fundamental change. It transforms our convictions and should be considered an important critical correction of our needs. It can have a truly transformative character because "education, real education, changes what people want."[4] Education is essentially about gaining insight into the nature of human beings. As in the "Evening," by Rainer Marie Rilke:

Slowly now the evening changes his garments
held for him by a rim of ancient trees;
you gaze: and the landscape divides and leaves you
one sinking and one rising toward the stars.

And you are left, to none belonging wholly,
not so dark as a silent house, nor quite
so surely pledged unto eternity
as that which grows to star and climbs the night.

To you is left (unspeakably confused)
your life, gigantic, ripening, full of fears,
so that it, now hemmed in, now grasping all,
is changed in you by turns to stone and stars.

This is a story of every human life summarized as a tension that accompanies our lives between the human and the divine, between earth and heaven. It describes our longing for something beyond ourselves, regardless of the idiosyncrasies of customs and cultures.[5] Following Rilke, we can say that our life is left to us. In order to understand the meaning and extent of the responsibility for living our own life, we must examine ourselves and answer the question of who we are and where are we going, as in Paul Gauguin's famous painting, "Where Do We Come From? What Are We? Where Are We Going?"

In modern societies education is seen as a kind of insurance policy. We speak of the instrumentalization of education in the "knowledge economy."

Education is reduced to useful knowledge which can be applied as need be. Worse still is the reduction of education to the formality of a certification, which stands for mastery and professionality in a given field of knowledge. Education in this sense has nothing to do with critical awareness and the desire to understand the complexity of one's life and life circumstances. We live under the tyranny of expertise that is connected with increasing specialization. Academia today is utterly confused about the task of education. What kind of education is still possible in industrial and global culture?

The Hermeneutic Teacher

The hermeneutics of education is not yet another method to be applied in an educational setting. Gadamer reminds us that it was "not my aim to investigate the theoretical foundation of work in [the human sciences] in order to put my findings to practical ends. My real concern was . . . not what we do or what we ought to do."[6] Hermeneutics should not be perceived as a tool which can be employed to achieve educational goals.[7] Rather, the hermeneutics of education thematizes the phenomenon of education as such and helps us to realize what is happening to us in the process of learning. Hermeneutics helps us to understand a non-calculative approach to education. The direct relevance of hermeneutics is in helping us to identify serious misconceptions and to address some unspoken premises that we often take for granted. For Gadamer, "hermeneutics is above all a praxis, the art of understanding and of making something understood to someone else. It is the heart of all education that wants to teach how to philosophize. In it what one has to exercise above all is the ear, the sensitivity for perceiving prior determinations, anticipations, and imprints that reside in concepts."[8] A thinking teacher is a model of the educator. In a process of education, what can be transferred is the testimony of our own thinking. Education is foremost about testimony, about sharing the experience of being human, sharing life, convictions, and knowledge. In its deepest existential sense, education is a call to transform our life by exercising openness toward the other and the unknown. It is an ethics of embracing the strange, the negative, without silencing the differences. In this respect education is about living diversity.

A hermeneutic account of education does not diminish the importance of the teacher. Instead it affects a shift from being the person responsible for the education of students to a person who sensitizes students, makes them aware of their capacity for self-education, and assists them in learning how to learn and progress toward self-understanding. The teacher has a profound responsibility of creating a learning relationship with students and encouraging them to build such relationships with others. One of the most characteristic features of this relationship is the openness to risk, misunderstanding, and the unexpected, which situates the relationship in the horizon between familiarity and strangeness.[9]

Gadamer's view on the importance of the teacher can be drawn from his remarks on the nature of hermeneutic philosophy: He writes: "Hermeneutic philosophy, as I envision it, does not understand itself as an absolute position but as a path of experiencing. Its modesty consists in the fact that for it there is no higher principle than this: holding oneself open to the conversation. This means, however, constantly recognizing in advance the possibility that your partner is right, even recognizing the possible superiority of your partner. Is this too little? This seems to me to be the only kind of integrity one can demand of a professor of philosophy—but it is one which one ought also to demand."[10] Hermeneutic education addresses the tension between epistemology and ontology and situates understanding in the realm of Heidegger's transcendental analytic of the hermeneutic conditions of the possibility of intelligible experience. Since understanding is the basic horizon in which we live our lives, and not primarily a particular activity of human beings, hermeneutic education concerns the disclosure and concealment of human experience. "Hermeneutic work is based on a polarity of familiarity and strangeness. . . . There is a tension. It is in the play between the traditionary text's strangeness and familiarity to us, between being a historically intended, distanciated object and belonging to a tradition. *The true locus of hermeneutics is this in-between.*"[11] By encountering the strange and the unfamiliar, the familiar is changed. The transformation of what is to be understood is the event of understanding.

The dialectic of familiarity and strangeness describes the way we live our lives and expresses our belonging to the world through experiences of affirmation and comfort as well as disorientation and alienation. Gadamer's hermeneutics of Dasein makes us aware that negativity and estrangement are not experiences to be eliminated. Rather, he invites us to perceive them as the very conditions that make understanding possible. Like the tension between the past and the present within historical consciousness, "the hermeneutic task consists in not covering up this tension by attempting a naive assimilation of the two but in consciously bringing it out."[12] The hermeneutic circle, which describes the constant interplay between the whole and the part, between what we understand and what we discover anew, plays a significant role in the hermeneutics of education. Any learning is the interplay of the familiar and the unknown. The experience of learning is a dialectical interchange with a circular structure. The event of education follows the dialectical structure of question and answer. Prejudices concern our knowledge of the whole; in being questioned they are understood, transforming our knowledge of the whole and paving the way for subsequent understanding. New knowledge is always conditioned by prior learning and is a continuous interplay between the familiar and the unknown.

Since self-understanding is a principal task of hermeneutics, affirming the freedom of the self requires the freedom of the other. Education, as with any interpersonal activity, presupposes the freedom of the students. Education that neglects or limits such freedom is, hermeneutically speaking, ethically dubious. The intersubjectivity of the process makes us aware of our responsibility for the other's freedom. Education is not only a liberation from but a liberation to, following the distinction between negative and positive freedom. Education is liberation from oneself toward a new self that is free from narrow-mindedness and self-absorption. In the educational setting we recognize the responsibility to the other, who is discovered in its irreducibility as someone weak and vulnerable. The sense of ethical responsibility, following Paul Ricoeur, is rooted in the recognition of the primacy of the subject's freedom as a premise for respecting the freedom of the other. As Gadamer says: "It is truly a tremendous task which faces every human every moment. His prejudices—his being saturated with wishes, drives, hopes, and interests—must be held under control to such an extent that the other is not made invisible or does not remain invisible. It is not easy to acknowledge that the other could be right, that oneself and one's own interests could be wrong."[13] The role of a teacher is to enhance the ethical intelligence of the students by helping them make ethical choices without having a totalizing power over the student. Education, like ethics, is not an abstract idea, but is an activity with a purpose. Instead of claiming that it is a goal-oriented action, we can say that it is a good-oriented action.[14] Education can be understood as a kind of assistance in the transformation of the self in the better living of life.

We experience inspiration through the example of the teacher. Education is about the continual presence of the teacher in the life of the students, and assisting them in familiarizing themselves with their ways of being-in-the-world.[15] As a *modus vivendi* of the teacher and the students, education requires open minds and generous hearts. "The loving person does not love the other because of the previous recognition of the values of the other person. On the contrary, only because one loves the other, one is able to recognize the valuable characteristics of the other person. Those characteristics would have to remain unrecognizable to an emotionally neutral, purely theoretical observation."[16] According to Gustav Siewerth and Otto Bolnow, education is always a venture of risk whose final outcome cannot be calculated and an engagement of free persons: "in education a free being is approaching another free being in a challenging way."[17]

Understanding Life and Taking Responsibility for Action

Following Heidegger's notion of understanding, we can emphasize that understanding is primarily a mode of Dasein's being-in-the-world. In Gadamer's words, "Heidegger's temporal analytics of Dasein has, I think, shown convincingly that understanding is not just one of the various possible behaviors of the subject but the mode of being of Dasein itself. It is in this sense that the term 'hermeneutics' has been used here. It denotes the basic being-in-motion of Dasein that constitutes its finitude and historicity, and hence embraces the whole of its experience of the world. Not caprice, or even an elaboration of a single aspect, but the nature of the thing itself makes the movement of understanding comprehensive and universal."[18] Understanding happens in the particularity of human existence, and "is not a resigned ideal of human experience. . . . Understanding is the original characteristic of the being of human life itself."[19] Hermeneutically speaking, education corresponds dialectically to the projection of our own-most possibilities. A world of unlimited imaginative variation is to be inhabited by the participants in education. Similar to Ricoeur's concept of refiguration, in which reading becomes a synthetic act that brings unity to the discordant experiences of temporal existence, education is about the student's identification with narrative meaning. The student's understanding of the subject matter is a dynamic process of appropriating the possible world that is opened up by the narrative. What happens here is the transformation of being a subject of education to becoming the narrator of one's own story. Understanding the subject matter becomes the student's self-understanding. The dynamics of application makes the student into the author of one's own story, which requires a creative translation of what wants to be understood into a personal project. At this point we can speak of a transition from narrative to ethics. Fundamental to ethical self-understanding is the notion of freedom. Freedom is a project that can only be fulfilled by action, not by discourse. For Ricoeur, "The whole problem of ethics is born from the question, what does it mean for someone to attest his freedom? It means to devote oneself to doing and not seeing. Therefore it is the whole problem of an appropriation by means of the work."[20] The ethical desire to live a good life can mature only in the horizon of freedom as the dialogical positioning of freedom in the second person. "You are" entails "you can."

Following Gadamer, all understanding is self-understanding. The hermeneutics of education makes us aware of the relationship between understanding the subject matter and understanding the self. Indeed, we can say that education is fundamentally about helping us in our search for self-understanding, and where "there is no self-understanding that is not mediated by signs, symbols, and texts."[21] In the process of education, the reflecting subject learns to gain meaningful access to one's own existence through this detour.[22] Knowledge is not about being pragmatic in the sense of being more adjustable to the world of economics. It is about becoming more human through self-knowledge. In the eighteenth century, Herder already challenged the Enlightenment's striving for technical perfection by emphasizing the importance of "cultivating the human." As Gadamer remarks: "Certainly there is knowledge involved in this real moral relationship, and so it is that love gives insight. But sympathy is much more than simply a condition of knowledge. Through it another person is transformed at the same time. Droysen makes the profound remark: 'You must be like that, for that is the way I love you': the secret of all education."[23]

Education becomes self-education in a process of purifying our thoughts and desires. In a dialogical relationship with others we learn to see ourselves in a different light. Following Gadamer again, we can say that one truly learns only through conversation. Education as self-education involves learning to deal with one's sympathies and antipathies and with the different aspects of social life. It awakens the desire to learn and to develop sensitivity toward that which one desires to know. This sensitivity can only be partially acquired by learning a particular discipline, and develops through practical application in interactions with others. Conversation is this horizon in which we learn sensitivity toward others in the act of trying to understand them. Being open to conversation means accepting new experiences from which we may learn. Conversation reshapes the lives of its participants into a state of permanent self-examination and renewal. Like the task of learning a foreign language, where our overriding goal is to converse with others and not merely acquire a range of technical skills, education involves cultivating a sympathetic disposition and understanding of the other and oneself.

Education is directed primarily toward educating oneself. Cultivation and formation (*Bildung*) means self-cultivation. Learning to speak is less about acquiring linguistic skills than the communicative relationship with others, and especially about feeling at home or making oneself at home in the world. Gadamer makes us aware that this is predominantly a process of self-education: "It is a self-education, such as I detect especially in the satisfaction that one has as a child or adolescent in trying out things, when one begins by imitation to use words one does not yet quite understand. Finally one manages to say it properly and then one is proud and joyful. Starting from these first observations we must proceed so that we never forget that we educate ourselves, that humanity educates itself, and that the so-called educator participates in this process only in such modest roles, for example, as teacher and as mother."[24] Education corrects and transforms our self-understanding. Since human beings are not isolated individuals, we realize that fulfilling the call to live a good life lies in the quality of our relationships. Education is therefore concerned with the way we live with the other in the world that we share. If we understand the human being as a spiritual being, with a longing for love, truth, beauty, and happiness, then any reduction in the scope and role of education to the simple transfer of knowledge and information in the development of marketable skills is a fatal mistake which is unfortunately widespread in our success-driven society. Education cannot be manufactured and should not aim at producing something measurable.[25] Pestalozzi describes the task of early education as "not a perfection in the accomplishments of the school, but fitness for life; not the acquisition of habits of blind obedience and of prescribed diligence, but a preparation for interdependent action."[26] When we listen to Paul's hymn to charity (1 Cor. 12.31–13.13), we realize that perfection does not consist in possessing exceptional qualities, but in charity, agape. It is a revealing insight.[27] It shows that education means growing toward understanding oneself and learning about the mysteries of the world in which we live. Paraphrasing Paul, we can say that a good teacher "does not boast, does not puff up with pride," but "rejoices in truth." For Gadamer, "a person who has to make moral decisions has always already learned something. He has been so formed by education and custom that he knows in general what is right. The task of making a moral decision is that of doing the right thing in a particular situation—i.e., seeing what is right within the situation and grasping it. He too has to act, choosing the right means, and his conduct must be governed just as carefully as that of the craftsman."[28] Education is about discovering life and unveiling the meaning of life, looking beyond ourselves and our self-regarding pursuits. It involves constant improvement, taking risks, and learning to act despite danger. Having been confronted with the pain and sorrow of our history, we are reminded that we are temporary residents of this world. The accumulation of wealth or information is always subject to loss, yet what cannot be taken from us is our self-understanding and the sense of personal integrity.

Education is as much about trying to understand oneself as to be understood. In this sense, education as self-education is an education toward sensitivity to life and a protest against indifference. By giving meaning to life, we not only overcome the temptation to indifference but share with others in the experience of changing the world. Elie Wiesel expressed this in a powerful way: "The opposite of love is not hate, it's indifference. The opposite of art is not ugliness, it's indifference. The opposite of faith is not heresy, it's indifference. And the opposite of life is not death, it's indifference." The highest task of education is to promote sensitivity to life by promoting understanding with others and the overcoming of indifference, ignorance, cynicism, and unawareness. In this respect, education is more about awakening our own initiative to take responsibility for our life and not to surrender to the requirements of any given educational system. Living a good life is the best proof of educational success, not an academic record from an established school or program.

Essential to all education is the practice of living one's life with others. Hermeneutics teaches us that understanding as the basic mode of human existence is less a theoretical matter than a practical task which we must responsibly exercise. Education is also an invitation to dialogue, a critical and self-critical taking into account of different perspectives. Such dialogue is not about exercising power over the other or over the matter that is to be understood, in the sense of reducing the task of understanding to a problem that needs to be solved. Hermeneutic education challenges the ideal of problem-solving and technical know-how. One of the most important features of education is understanding the student not as an observer but as an active and critical participant in the educational process. This process can be described as an unfolding inquiry in which the dialectic of question and answer allows for an understanding both of the matter that needs to be understood and of the self. For Gadamer, one learns only through such conversation. Like any genuine conversation, the participants in education learn by listening to each other, and in this respect education promotes a culture of listening.[29] In a true conversation we situate the understanding of the other in the horizon of our own understanding: "This openness always includes our situating the other meaning in relation to the whole of our own meanings or ourselves in relation to it."[30] Accepting ourselves is the only way to accept and welcome the other. As Gadamer reminds us, "It is a widespread mistake to take tolerance to be a virtue which abandons insisting on one's own position and represents the other as equally valid. . . . It is rather one's own strength, especially the strength of one's own existential certainty, which permits one to be tolerant."[31] Education thus involves developing the capacity to form an opinion while encountering real differences and promoting the spirit of tolerance and community: "It is exactly the otherness, the recognition of our self, the re-encountering of the other, in language, art, religion, law, and history, which is able to guide us toward a true communality."[32] Education imposes a responsibility for continuous self-education. Taking responsibility for one's education requires building relationships with others. One's self-understanding matures in the context of developing self-understanding with others. We can therefore speak of the reciprocity of the educational process. Self-education is an openness to the influence of others and an acceptance of the responsibility of education as a continuous life task.

When Gadamer uses the Hegelian word "in-dwelling" (*einhausen*) to describe education as an existential effort in making oneself at home in the world, he brings into discussion the whole tension between being at home and homelessness, between self-possession and the uncertainty of understanding. It is an attempt to assist human beings in developing their at-homeness in everyday experience. Gadamer's concept of in-dwelling concerns not the domestication of the world we live in but an exposure to the dialectics of life with all its recurring interplay between revealing (*Entbergen*) and concealing (*Verbergen*).[33] Hermeneutic education is concerned not with intellectual processes alone but, following Heidegger, with understanding as the way of Dasein's being-in-the-world. What is happening in education is a transformation of the way we perceive ourselves and the world. It occurs by understanding our presuppositions and by opening ourselves radically toward the new. Understanding our presuppositions means that we question them and thus critically address what we already know. Fundamental to all learning is the hermeneutic virtue of openness. Because understanding is never final, the call to continuous education is transformational and ongoing. Prudence (*prudentia*) in an educational setting enables us to look ahead (*providere*) and prepare for life by promoting continuous self-education and not surrendering ourselves to the anxieties of life.

The Imperative of Self-Education

Understanding as the mode of our being-in-the-world is also a call to responsibility in the sense of an answer to the recognition of our existential possibilities. Our response expresses our interest (*inter-esse*) in the well-being of others. Understanding is a practical activity that demands from us an existential engagement. Following Gadamer, we can call this capacity of the human being to respond to the uniqueness of a given situation application or self-understanding. To understand oneself means to learn one's way around, which is the principal task of education. It is a call to openness toward the other and to a critical examination of our prejudices. It requires our courage in facing the critique of the other, which in turn causes a self-doubt which is not only unavoidable but a welcome corrective to the way we perceive ourselves. Distrusting our self-understanding teaches us to remain open to the strange and unfamiliar and to deal with the discomfort of critique. Vulnerability and openness to challenge and difference are decisive characteristics of a person, and they are all required in the educational process. The hermeneutics of education stresses the importance of learning how to lose. Referring to the experience of losing a game, Gadamer accentuates the close relation between the way we deal with difficult existential tasks and our openness toward the other.[34] This openness is the inevitable result of our willingness to engage ourselves in the hermeneutic tension between self-acceptance and self-questioning, between familiarity and disorientation, between feeling at home and being exiled.

Education is always an open project. It is a permanent call to self-education, which surprises us as we continue to respond to life's tasks. Gadamer reminds us that "as a rule we experience the course of events as something that continually changes our plans and expectations. Someone who tries to stick to his plans discovers precisely how powerless his reason is."[35] As well: "Thus experience is experience of human finitude. The truly experienced person is one who has taken this to heart, who knows that he is master neither of time nor the future. The experienced man knows that all foresight is limited and all plans uncertain. In him is realized the true value of experience. If it is characteristic of every phase of the process of experience that the experienced person acquires a new openness to new experiences, this is certainly true of the idea of being perfectly experienced. It does not mean that experience has ceased and a higher form of knowledge is reached (Hegel), but that for the first time experience fully and truly is. In it all dogmatism, which proceeds from the soaring desires of the human heart, reaches an absolute barrier. Experience teaches us to acknowledge the real. The genuine result of experience, then, as of all desire to know, is to know what is. But 'what is,' here, is not this or that thing, but 'what cannot be destroyed' (Ranke). Real experience is that whereby man becomes aware of his finiteness. In it are discovered the limits of the power and the self-knowledge of his planning reason."[36] Education thus involves understanding our intellectual finitude and may be very helpful in helping us deal with human finitude more generally. What is essential in the hermeneutics of education is understanding that knowledge cannot be separated from our mode of being. With reference to Aristotle's ethics and against the predominant ideal of objectification in modern science, Gadamer stresses the unity of what we are and what we know.[37] Hermeneutics aims not at propositional knowledge but at assisting human beings in their self-understanding and understanding of the human condition.

The hermeneutics of education makes us aware of the basic condition of human life and by this awareness teaches us to live our lives to the fullest. It is an education to responsibility and to confront our lives with maximal sensitivity to the question of what is essential to being a human being, which in turn leads to critical inquiry into living a meaningful life. Education cannot be separated from one's development as a human being. What is most at stake here are our own possibilities. Hermeneutic education as a lived understanding encourages the critical examination of the meaning of one's life.

When Pope Julius II asked the young Raphael to paint some frescos to decorate the Apostolic Palace, the painter depicted four fundamental disciplines: theology, philosophy, poetry, and jurisprudence. One of the most famous frescos in that series is the "School of Athens." They allegorically represent the historical continuity of Plato's Academy. Raphael painted not the real school but the perfect community of thinkers. The hermeneutic ideal of school is based on the hermeneutic gesture of hospitality. It concerns the community in which we experience the profundity of our temporal and finite existence. We can share with others what is most precious in us, our very existence which is absolutely unique. School becomes then a *genius loci*, where we can live through the mystery of our very being.

School symbolizes not a place where we accumulate information but the hermeneutic gesture of extending welcome, an invitation to experience the unity and wholeness of our being in the continuous task of interpreting our existence as a whole. School becomes a space where we can encounter our own life by embracing the inner tensions and share our experience with our fellow human beings. It becomes a journey that allows for the strange and unexpected. Confronting doubt and insecurity need not impede the educational experience. On the contrary, embracing the tension between illumination and concealment makes us aware of the very nature of hermeneutic truth and by encouraging challenge sensitizes us toward living the greater complexity of our life. In the process of education we critically examine life experience, an analysis that requires our active participation. Critical inquiry into our being-in-the-world cannot happen in isolation from the world we live in, nor from our very existence which is temporal and finite. Education as self-understanding concerns our experience in the world. The stress is on the mediation that happens in the process of education. A human being is a mediator between one's self-knowledge and knowledge of the world in which one lives. Education is always mediated in the sense of facilitating our experience of the world and shifting attention away from itself and to the greater whole of the life context that it accompanies.

Crucially important for the future of education are the origins, role, and character of our fore-conceptions. The meaningful life is more than the ability to strive for socially acclaimed success and achievement. If the hermeneutic ideal of education concerns life as a whole and the art of living to one's full potential, educational experience enables us to mature as human beings and creatively develop our self-understanding. Education is an existential task, a participation in the process of building a culture, and enables the individual to participate in the conversation that we are within the limits not only of our socio-cultural condition but of our understanding as finite human beings. Since we are born into socio-historical contexts that are saturated with meanings, we participate in the event of tradition. In fact, we are tradition in the sense of participating in meanings that have already been interpreted. Hermeneutics teaches us that while the human being is inextricably embedded in a socio-historical context, any interpretation needs to make explicit the historical and existential situation of the interpreter. In opposition to modern epistemological ideals, hermeneutics calls for liberation from the false promises of scientific objectification. It argues against disengagement of the thinking person from the matter to be thought and against any reduction of education to gaining control over life or to the ambition to manage, regulate, and order.

Conclusion

We live in a time when conflicting existential views coexist in a way never witnessed before, causing many to try to justify their personal views and their way of life. We can look at Kohelet, who attempted to reconcile the traditional faith in which he was brought up with the rapid changes in the world in which he lived. He had sufficient knowledge and intellectual courage to examine and critically question his tradition. He also proposed a way of arguing for the traditional faith, by demonstrating the futility of new approaches and encouraging the personal search for truth. Reading Kohelet, we might still be unable to find answers to many questions we are confronted with in our daily life, but we should not feel discouraged. There are no easy answers to the challenges of the unquiet human heart: "Making many books there is no end, and much study is a weariness of the flesh" (Eccl. 12.12). Nevertheless, when we carefully listen to Kohelet's teaching, we will find an intellectual and existential joy of searching. In this respect the journey proves important enough to invest our best energies. Gadamer expresses this notion of being on the way to a goal while speaking of the self-sufficiency of dreams: "Dreams will not be fulfilled. Their fulfillment occurs in themselves."[38] Education calls us to be wholly involved in, attentive and responsive to our existential situation.

The task of hermeneutic education might sound like a spiritual program of personal renewal following the call to permanent conversion rather than a quest for reform to well-established concepts of education in traditional institutions. However, in the continuous interplay between thought and action we realize that interpretation, understanding, and application are one unified process which situates us between reproduction and transformation, between authority and emancipation, and between trust and suspicion. Education shapes how we think, what we think about, and how we translate our thinking into the reality of our personal and social lives; it creates a horizon in which we discover the intensity of our own lives in relationship to others and share the meaning of life with them by transforming what is uniquely and unmistakably our own into something common to all. Genuine education contributes to the life and transformation of all involved. In that sense, education is not only about cultivating our own understanding, but through the work of self-refinement contributing to the transformation of the world.

Hermeneutic education reminds us that the only way to self-understanding and understanding the meaning of life is through lived experience. Pain and suffering, the experience of loss and deprivation, alienation and estrangement accompany us in the search for self-understanding. What we learn on that journey is that we are not independent and disengaged individuals. Educational virtues encourage us to face life in its integrity and to understand it as an existential project rather than focus on the desire for control and mastery alone. The scientific ideal describes our capacity to make, create, and plan, however individual efficacy is not about mastery over oneself, the other, or any matter to be understood. It is about disclosing the mystery of our life in all its aspects, including the tensions in our self-understanding.

As we participate in the hermeneutic conversation, we can say that we participate in the event of education.[39] Our lived understanding discloses the essential characteristics of human life in its temporality and finitude and thus reshapes our self-understanding by revealing the mystery of life in its entirety. The quality of the conversation depends far less on what we participants know about the subject matter. What is decisive is the understanding of who we are and want to become.

Notes

1 In German, *Pädagogik* is concerned with *paideia* as well as with the academic study of *paideia* (*Erziehungswissenschaft*) dealing with the theory and practice of education. Gadamer explores in detail the concept of *Bildung* in the opening chapter of *Truth and Method*. Following Hegel's understanding of *Bildung* as the duty to cultivate oneself to realize one's unique potential, Gadamer situates the understanding of *Bildung* in the horizon of responsibility "to keep oneself open to what is other, to other, more universal points of view." Hans-Georg Gadamer, *Truth and Method*, trans. Joel Weinsheimer and Donald G. Marshall (New York: Continuum, 2004), 17. *Bildung* is the attitude of mind, which forms one's sensibility and character.

2 Hans-Georg Gadamer, "Dialectic and Sophism in Plato's Seventh Letter," *Dialogue and Dialectic: Eight Hermeneutical Studies on Plato*, trans. P. Christopher Smith (New Haven: Yale University Press, 1980), 117.

3 "To the extent that learning is logically a broader category than reading, it offers a more appropriate paradigm for a universal hermeneutics." Shaun Gallagher, *Hermeneutics and Education* (Albany: State University of New York Press, 1992), 331.

4 Michael Ventimiglia, "Three Educational Orientations: A Peircean Perspective on Education and the Growth of the Self," *Studies in Philosophy and Education* (2005) 24: 291–308, 308.

5 For Gadamer, "an education by art becomes an education to art. Instead of art's preparing us for true moral and political freedom, we have the culture of an 'aesthetic state,' a cultured society (*Bildungsgesellschaft*) that takes an interest in art." Gadamer, *Truth and Method*, 351.

6 Gadamer, *Truth and Method*, xxviii.

7 Cf. Peter Sotioru, Ann Berthoff, and Timothy Crusius's work on the possibility of applying Gadamer's hermeneutics to the educational setting. Peter Sotioru, "Articulating a Hermeneutic Pedagogy: The Philosophy of Interpretation," *Journal of Advanced Composition* 13 (2) (1993), 365-80; Timothy W Crusius, *A Teacher's Introduction to Philosophical Hermeneutics* (Urbana: National Council of Teachers of English, 1991); Ann E. Berthoff, "Rhetoric as Hermeneutics." *College Composition and Communication* 42 (1991), 279-87.

8 Hans-Georg Gadamer, "Reflections on my Philosophical Journey," in Lewis Edwin Hahn, ed., *The Philosophy of Hans-Georg Gadamer* (Chicago: Open Court, 1997), 17.

9 "To recognize one's own in the alien, to become at home in it, is the basic movement of spirit, whose being consists only in returning to itself from what is other. Hence all theoretical *Bildung*, even acquiring foreign languages and conceptual worlds, is merely the continuation of a process of *Bildung* that begins much earlier. Every single individual who raises himself out of his natural being to the spiritual finds in the language, customs, and institutions of his people a pre-given body of material which, as in learning to speak, he has to make his own. Thus every individual is always engaged in the process of *Bildung* and in getting beyond his naturalness, inasmuch as the world into which he is growing is one that is humanly constituted through language and custom. . . . Thus what constitutes the essence of *Bildung* is clearly not alienation as such, but the return to oneself, which presupposes alienation, to be sure. However, *Bildung* is not to be understood only as the

process of historically raising the mind to the universal; it is at the same time the element within which the educated man (*Gebildete*) moves." Gadamer, *Truth and Method*, 13.

10 Gadamer, "Reflections on my Philosophical Journey," 36.

11 Gadamer, *Truth and Method*, 295.

12 Gadamer, *Truth and Method*, 305.

13 Hans-Georg Gadamer, *On Education, Poetry, and History: Applied Hermeneutics*, ed. Dieter Misgeld and Graeme Nicholson, trans. Lawrence Schmidt and Monica Reuss (Albany: State University of New York Press, 1992), 233.

14 "The mark of a prudent man [is] to be able to deliberate rightly about what is good and what is advantageous for himself; not in particular respects, e.g., what is good for health or physical strength, but what is conducive to the good life generally." Aristotle, *Nicomachean Ethics*, trans. James A. K. Thomson (London: Penguin, 2004), 150.

15 Cf. William F. Pinar and William M. Reynolds, eds., *Understanding Curriculum as Phenomenological and Deconstructed Text* (New York: Teachers College Press, 1992).

16 Gustav Siewerth, *Wagnis und Bewahrung: Zur metaphysischen Begründung des erzieherischen Auftrages* (Düsseldorf, Schwann, 1958). See also Otto Friedrich Bollnow, *Existenzphilosophie und Pädagogik: Versuch über unstetige Formen der Erziehung* (Stuttgart: Kohlhammer, 1984), 106: "Der Liebende liebt nicht, weil er zuvor die Werte des andern Menschen erkannt hätte, sondern umgekehrt, nur weil er liebt, ist er imstande, diejenigen wertvollen Eigenschaften des andern Menschen zu entdecken, die einer gefühlsmäßig neutralen, rein theoretischen Betrachtung unerkennbar bleiben müßten."

17 "[Der] eigentliche Kern der Erziehung . . . darauf beruht, daß hier ein freies Wesen einem andern freien Wesen fordernd entgegentritt." Bollnow, *Existenzphilosophie und Pädagogik*, 133–4.

18 Gadamer, *Truth and Method*, xxvii.

19 Gadamer, *Truth and Method*, 250.

20 Paul Ricoeur, "The Problem of the Foundation of Moral Philosophy," trans. David Pellauer, *Philosophy Today* 22, (3) (Fall 1978), 177. For Ricoeur, the concept of "the primacy of the ethics of the good over the morality of obligation," narrative and ethics are inseparable and indispensable.

21 Paul Ricoeur, *From Text to Action: Essays in Hermeneutics II*, trans. Kathleen Blamey and John B. Thompson (Evanston: Northwestern University Press, 1991), 15.

22 Cf. Andrzej Wiercinski, "Hermeneutics and the Indirect Path to Understanding," in Edward Fiala, Dariusz Skórczewski, and Andrzej Wiercinski, eds., *Interpreting the Self: Hermeneutics, Psychoanalysis, and Literary Studies* (Lublin: Katolicki Uniwersytet Lubelski, 2009), 11–44.

23 Gadamer, *Truth and Method*, 226–7.

24 Hans-Georg Gadamer, "Education Is Self-Education," *Journal of Philosophy of Education* 35 (4) (2002), 529-38, 530. Gadamer presented his address "Erziehung ist Sich-Erziehen," at the Dietrich Bonhoeffer Gymnasium, Eppelheim, on May 19, 1999, three months into his hundredth year.

25 Cf. Andrzej Wiercinski, "Non-Calculative Responsibility: Martin Heidegger's and Paul Ricoeur's Hermeneutics of Responsibility," in Marcelino Agís Villaverde, Carlos Beliñas Fernándes, Fernanda Henriques, and Jesús Ríos Vicente, eds., *Herméneutica y responsibilidad: Homenaje a Paul Ricoeur* (Santiago de Compostela: Universidade, Servizo de Publicatión e Intercambio Científico, 2005), 413-32.

26 Johann H. Pestalozzi, *Letters on Early Education and James P. Greaves*, Letter XXI, February 4, 1819.

27 "Insight is more than the knowledge of this or that situation. It always involves an escape from something that had deceived us and held us captive. Thus insight always involves an element of self-knowledge and constitutes a necessary side of what we called experience in the proper sense. Insight is something we come to. It too is ultimately part of the vocation of man, i.e., to be discerning and insightful." Gadamer, *Truth and Method*, 350.

28 Gadamer, *Truth and Method*, 314–15.

29 "In human relations the important thing is, as we have seen, to experience the Thou truly as a Thou, i.e., not to overlook his claim but to let him really say something to us. Here is where openness belongs. But ultimately this openness does not exist only for the person who speaks; rather, anyone who listens is fundamentally open. Without such openness to

one another there is no genuine human bond. Belonging together always also means being able to listen to one another. When two people understand each other, this does not mean that one person 'understands' the other. Similarly, 'to hear and obey someone' does not mean simply that we do blindly what the other desires. We call such a person slavish. Openness to the other, then, involves recognizing that I myself must accept some things that are against me, even though no one else forces me to do so." Gadamer, *Truth and Method,* 355.

[30] Gadamer, *Truth and Method,* 271.

[31] Gadamer, *On Education, Poetry, and History,* 206.

[32] Gadamer, *On Education, Poetry, and History,* 235.

[33] "But this [Dasein's understanding itself in its being] self-understanding [*Selbstverständnis*] in all its forms, the extreme opposite of self-consciousness [*Selbstbewusstesein*] and self-possession [*Selbstbesitz*]. Rather, it is an understanding that always places itself in question, which is not only grounded on the 'mine-ness' of my being that is revealed in the possibility of death, but at the same time encompasses all recognition of oneself in the other, which first opens up in dialogue." Hans-Georg Gadamer, "Letter to Dallmayr," in Diane P. Michelfelder and Richard E. Palmer, eds., *Dialogue and Deconstruction: The Gadamer-Derrida Encounter* (Albany: State University of New York Press, 1989), 95.

[34] Cf. Rudolf Bernet, "Gadamer on the Subject's Participation in the Game of Truth," *The Review of Metaphysics* 58 (4) (June 2005), 785-814.

[35] Gadamer, *Truth and Method,* 365.

[36] Gadamer, *Truth and Method,* 351.

[37] "We spoke of the interpreter's belonging to the tradition he is interpreting, and we saw that understanding itself is a historical event. The alienation of the interpreter from the interpreted by the objectifying methods of modern science, characteristic of the hermeneutics and historiography of the nineteenth century, appeared as the consequence of a false objectification. My purpose in returning to the example of Aristotelian ethics is to help us realize and avoid this. For moral knowledge, as Aristotle describes it, is clearly not objective knowledge, i.e., the knower is not standing over against a situation that he merely observes; he is directly confronted with what he sees. It is something that he has to do." Gadamer, *Truth and Method,* 312.

[38] Hans-Georg Gadamer, *Philosophische Lehrjahre* (Frankfurt: Vittorio Klostermann, 1977), 59.

[39] In the process of education, like in any other conversation, we express our personal views, values, and preferences. Cf. Laurillard's conversational model of education, Diana Laurillard, *Rethinking University Teaching* (London: Routledge, 2002).

Chapter 8

Education and Exemplars: On Learning to Doubt the Overman

Babette Babich

There are no educators.

—*Nietzsche*

Out of School: Education and Scholarship from Ivan Illich to Friedrich Nietzsche

In what follows I treat Ivan Illich's *Deschooling Society*[1] as a general prelude to a discussion of Nietzsche's philosophical engagement with his classical philology, a profession which he argued to be essentially pedagogical, one of a piece with cultural formation, understood as Nietzsche liked to put it as actively "getting" oneself a culture. Such cultivation is antithetical to the "schooling" Illich criticizes. I then take this educational point further by exploring the notion of the exemplar for Nietzsche[2] as he analyses it in "Schopenhauer as Educator." I conclude with a critical reading (or philologically contextual "de-schooling") of the standard understanding of the meaning, the *who*, of Nietzsche's *Übermensch.*

Illich challenges the institution of the Western educational ideal of school as such. He means by this the entirety of the educational system including its structural design, its standards, and its legitimacy or authority. School on Illich's reading is so consummately Western that it functions as the most expedient if also inherently innocuous instrument of globalization. As Jacques Ellul observes, schooling "indoctrinates"; it does not encourage critically reflective thinking.[3] Just as contemporary philosophy celebrates what it designates as *critical thinking*—which is never thinking otherwise than in accord with established conviction (only more insistently)—intellectuals, so Ellul argues, are the most thoroughly indoctrinated of all.[4] Where Ellul discusses the technical dimensions of education in terms of the formation of public belief and intellectual conviction, Illich anticipates the dark contradictions of the current crises of globalization where school in its current form fails to function as intended and nonetheless can neither be dispensed with nor substantively redesigned. The problem with school in the United States and elsewhere was that it was *not working*, but still more of the same was everywhere touted as a remedy. "If it teaches nothing else, school teaches the value of escalation: the value of the American way of doing things." "The Vietnam war fits the logic of the moment. Its success has been measured by the numbers of persons effectively treated by cheap bullets delivered at immense cost, and this brutal calculus is unashamedly called 'body count.' Just as business is business, the never-ending accumulation of money, so war is killing, the never-ending accumulation of dead bodies. In like manner, education is schooling, and this open-ended process is counted in pupil-hours. The various processes are irreversible and self-justifying. By economic standards the country gets richer and richer. By death-accounting standards the nation goes on winning its war forever. And by school standards the population becomes increasingly educated." "School programs hunger for progressive intake of instruction, but even if the hunger leads to steady absorption, it never yields the joy of knowing something to one's satisfaction. Each subject comes packaged with the instruction to go on consuming one 'offering' after another, and last year's wrapping is always obsolete for this year's consumer. The textbook racket builds on this demand. Educational reformers promise each new generation the latest and the best, and the public is schooled into demanding."[5]

Like Jacques Ellul's discussions of technology,[6] the claim Illich seeks to make is systematic in the strongest sense. Thus he asks us to consider education in the social context, including political and military interests as well as class and economic concerns. For the educational ideal promised as a result of schooling—and this is what educators to this day continue to tell their charges—is far less about learning than it highlights Western consumption. An education is the royal road of access to the same and what education is not about is what Illich calls a "life of action" (a life, to follow Dorothy Day, of *service*). Like his fellow-Viennese, Karl Kraus, who mocked psychoanalysis to the face of its founder, Sigmund Freud, by naming it the disease whose cure it purports to be, Illich argues that schooling is the solution to a problem invented by school itself. Illich maintained his own focus on the integrated system that "today's futuristic planners seek to make economically feasible what is technically possible while refusing to face the inevitable social consequence: the increased craving of all men for goods and services that will remain the privilege of a few."[7] There is no getting out of the circle of avarice (what we politely name "consumption") or its ineluctable (which we less politely choose to ignore) contradictions: "The established teachers unions, the technological wizards, and the educational liberation movement reinforce the commitment of the entire society to the fundamental axioms of a schooled world, somewhat in the manner in which many peace and protest movements reinforce the commitments of their members—be they black, female, young, or poor—to seek justice through the growth of the gross national income."[8]

Although we are accustomed to bracket Nietzsche's economic views, he too lamented the loss of the higher "capital of every citizen's heart and head,"[9] riches of the heart and the mind literally sacrificed to political involvements and thus to be accounted in addition to the financial costs of war. Later, Nietzsche's Zarathustra urges: "O my brothers, I dedicate and direct you to a new nobility: you shall become procreators and cultivators and sowers of the future—verily, not to a nobility that you might buy like shopkeepers with shopkeepers' gold; for whatever has its price has little value" (Z, *Old and New Tablets*, §12).

The point Illich seeks to make throughout his influential but ill-understood *Deschooling Society* is the point he sought to make throughout his career. It is the reason that Illich is able to honor not only one of his inspirations for his thinking on education, Paulo Freire,[10] but Ellul as well.[11]

This point of reception (i.e., Friere and Ellul but also others some have heard of and other sources invoked without having been read, as in the case of a certain antique origin for the coinage of Nietzsche's overman as we shall detail below) is key in what follows for understanding Illich's critical challenge to the contemporary schema of education or schooling. The reception of ideas is part not only of philosophy as dialogue (in Gadamer's sense as conversation)[12] but of cultivation in its broadest sense as what the French name a formation; it is this Nietzsche intends at the end of his life when he speaks of "one who has turned out well" (EH, *Why I am so wise*, §2).

Schooling Society

This chapter is as much about Nietzsche as it is about Illich, although Illich is indispensable as our point of departure, and that is for a number of reasons. By contrast with Nietzsche's formative ideal, we academics and educators *live* on the terms of Illich's thoroughly "schooled" society. We do not merely "make our living" thereby, and as educators we do not school the school, but we are schooled by it. At its best, its educational ideal might aspire to *paideia*, to borrow the title of Werner Jaeger's three volumes on Greek culture,[13] and this admittedly "high" aspiration (in the sense of high-mindedness and in the sense of higher culture and even higher incomes) drives an Ivy League sensibility as this is sometimes enshrined in the "great books" tradition in the United States (always limited to private institutions, and then mostly to those that take themselves very seriously indeed). Thus levels of education and culture (which is, once again, a matter not of culture but of money)[14] are distinguished together with the further educational metaphor of "progress" (from *lower* to *higher*).[15]

What is patent is that scholarship at the same "higher" or university levels of schooling reflects (no matter whether suffered or enjoyed) *conventional* wisdom. This is the received or mainstream view, just to the extent that this view reflects and is limited to the scholars (and the scholarship) popularly cited and referenced—and only these. Thus the current chapter is already problematic to the extent that it begins with Illich who inevitably leaves most theorists and philosophers of education discomfited simply because he questions the institution itself. Illich's brief is abolition, not reform—a dissonant project for a former university rector and for one who taught at universities and who lectured to academics inside and out of school all his life.[16]

Illich—like Kraus, like Nietzsche—writes to provoke. Indeed, and although I call myself a friend of the late Ivan Illich (of the telephone and letter variety: we never met in person), I too find his views unsettling. I have yet to recover from the shock of reading (just reading) *H2O and the Waters of Forgetfulness*[17] and I have yet to stop teaching it in my classes on technology and environmental ethics just because of its uncanny rightness (and for the same disturbing reasons). In addition to being unsettlingly, dissonantly right, Illich is also routinely one-sided (this does not diminish his argument, though it is a hermeneutic aid to understanding it). He was often wrong, notably and excessively so, about women, for one example (but so was Baudrillard and so was Bataille), etc. If Nietzsche escapes the list it is because he knew this about himself and named it so—not by calling these his "views" much less his opinions, *but* by naming these, his incorrigible convictions, his "down deep" and "unteachable stupidity" (BGE §231).

To Illich, we may add writers like Theodor Adorno but also Herbert Marcuse and even Martin Heidegger as those who lament the consequences of today's now-well-sedimented tradition of standard cultivation. For education has indeed become increasingly "institutionalized," to use Illich's language, and the school is more and more rather than less and less an instrument of the same "propaganda" Ellul diagnoses in several texts. This extends to the passion for computerizing classrooms at every level from kindergarten to the university and can be seen in the proliferation of power-point presentations as the universal medium of instruction.[18] Most discussions of this phenomenon (including Illichs's) focus on grade school, thus it can help to point to pre-school and to the media success of programs like Sesame Street. Illich's key point, however, is that it is the learner who learns and yet, and by way of a dangerous metonymy, the institution (or the teacher) claims the credit for it,[19] only to end, as Nietzsche says in another context, exemplifying the very way metonymy functions, by believing, as educators, in "the" truth of this claim.

For Illich, importantly Heideggerian here, we always come to what learning we do in a hermeneutic context that always and already pre-exists the specific occasion. Learning in order to be learning always has a reference to this context (and to abstract from this pregiven context is to slow down or eliminate learning altogether). But Illich eschews fancy terms, deglamorizing school and deconstructing its achievements. The skills that are involved—reading, writing, calculating, even philosophizing—are skills that can be gotten by "training," perhaps with a tutor or expert who points one in the right direction, but also and perhaps on one's own. Learning a language is Illich's favorite example for such skills are always gotten in spite of rather than because of school. The teacher at any level, including Socrates himself as Plato knew, is reduced to a tutorial adjunct to the learner.

Whereas Plato's example is full of mythical references to *lēthe* as the draught that brings the soul to forget its pre-existent life mixed with enough mathematics to keep the reader on his or her toes (the doubled square, the triangulated or squared circle, the square root of 2), Illich refers to Freire's empirical and pragmatic discovery "that any adult can begin to read in a matter of forty hours if the first words he deciphers are charged with political meaning. Freire trains his teachers to move into a village and to discover the words which designate current important issues, such as the access to a well or the compound interest on the debts owed to the *patron*. In the evening the villagers meet for the discussion of these key words. They begin to realize that each word stays on the blackboard even after its sound has faded. The letters continue to unlock reality and to make it manageable as a problem."[20]

As a technological 'system', in Ellul's sense, Illich points out that the assumptions in education are consequently systematic: "the more treatment there is, the better are the results; or, escalation leads to success. The pupil is thereby 'schooled' to confuse teaching with learning, grade advancement with education, a diploma with competence, and fluency with the ability to say something new. His imagination is 'schooled' to accept service in place of value. Medical treatment is mistaken for health care, social work for the improvement of community life, police protection for safety, military poise for national security, the rat race for productive work. Health, learning, dignity, independence, and creative endeavor are defined as little more than the performance of the institutions which claim to serve these ends, and their improvement is made to depend on allocating more resources to the management of hospitals, schools, and other agencies in question."[21]

There is a lot said here and a lot of it is politically (because economically and socially) controversial. But on a purely philosophical level, what Illich says also illustrates that he happens to have had (as Nietzsche had, as Heidegger had, as Adorno had but also as Ellul had had),[22] conspicuously rigorous standards for what will count as learning or culture. To see Illich's point and to comprehend its scope requires a lifetime, as Aristotle had already emphasized for the judgment on the felicity of a life, or as in this case, a programmatic formulation regarding "schooling" or education. The Canadian Thomist and Jesuit, Bernard Lonergan similarly emphasizes the importance not of teaching but much rather and only of learning.[23]

How We Become What We Are: On Getting Ourselves a Culture

Illich's indictment of the contemporary monopoly of the educational institution (which has long been in the United States a corporate, i.e., a business and private rather than a public, affair) was for its part meant to advocate on behalf of the individual learner or auto-didact, which, and to be sure, Illich already held the student to be in any case.

Thus Illich points to the substitution of credentials for competence. The student who, for example, hopes to work to develop alternative environmental practices or in medicine or business or even education (by which last one mostly means teaching at a grade or high school and *not* a university level) seeks to train at programs that purport to teach the same. But (here to be ruthless and to stay with the first named example and thus with the recently branded environmental studies programs that now abound in our universities and colleges): to say that such programs "teach" what they purport to teach is only to say that they have been certified to certify, providing the necessary degree or certificate which degree or certificate may or may not suffice in the securing of a job in the student's chosen career.[24] Or consider the assumption we seem unable to do without or to challenge: that a letter of recommendation or a degree tells us what a potential student (or colleague) might be able to do, that is, that such certifying documents authentically attest to competence much less talent.[25]

Talk about education, philosophical or otherwise, is usually talk about educating others. Hence I have invoked the kind of jobs for which a university professor's students tend to be "educated." But what about the life of the university educator, what about the academic's life? It may be easier to see the problem as one that bears on the *educator* as well as on the *educated* if we modify (in a Heideggerian spirit) Illich's own second and third chapters moving from the "Phenomenology of School" to the "Ritualization of Progress," via a reading of Nietzsche on philology addressed to his own philological colleagues. What is at stake is the substitution of the letter (here: the ritual proceeding of schooling) for the spirit (i.e., for learning or cultivation). Thus Nietzsche addresses the scientific or theoretical foundations of classical scholarship.

Nietzsche begins his 1869 inaugural lecture at Basel in a classic Ciceronian fashion by circumscribing his topic as an address to philologists on philology. Thus he adverts to the classical profession of classics (which he calls, because he is speaking German: *Philologie*), noting the historical and not less the cultural, by which he means *educational*, directionality of the field itself: "philology at every period from its origin onwards was at the same time pedagogical."[26]

Nietzsche's first offence in a small flurry of offenses contra the classical sensibility of his own profession (including, most grievously for his future at Basel, his own colleagues) was to *begin* by appealing not to the scholar but the *artist* and to "others of artistic minds," and to do so for the sake of the latter's "judgment"[27] just because the philological expert or scientific scholar would himself be making very specific stylistic judgments of his own.

Characterizing the exemplary application of such stylistic matters as a programmatically Kantian *critique* of scholarly judgment, Nietzsche's Basel lecture focuses on the quintessentially classical "Homer question," a tradition going back not only to Goethe and Schiller but the famed first philologist Friedrich August Wolf and still more, as Nietzsche underscores this, to the philological tradition formed by the ancients themselves.[28] Beginning with a return to the ancient institution of a *contest* between Homer and Hesiod and indeed Peisistratus, Nietzsche outlines the standard Homer question as "the question concerning Homer as a personality,"[29] that is, the question of the personal existence and the person *per se* of Homer. But the Homer question, qua question, is a question already roundly answered, multiply and canonically so. This was the case in Nietzsche's day and long before and it remains so today. From a scholarly point of view, the Homer question is a question long since dissolved *as* a question.

Regarded hermeneutically,[30] Nietzsche's inaugural ambition seems bent on resuscitating the "Homer question" by recalling it "as a question" to the philologists themselves. But this is not quite his aim, and in the course of his lecture Nietzsche unpacks a technical examination of the subjective foundations of the objective question, that is to say, the very Kantian matter of "aesthetic" judgment in philological scholarship or science. In this same critical fashion, Nietzsche raises the question of style as the distinctively reflexive question of scholarly "taste" now articulated as a literally *scientific* question.[31]

Instructively enough, we note that it is by means of stylistic attributes that the scholar identifies or "distinguishes" works of art or literary texts, attributing works of sculpture or pottery to this or that era, this or that artist, classifying jewelry, temple offerings, cylindrical seals, and so on. Similarly scholars characterize literary works—poetry, philosophy, history—in terms of style and at the same time a number of these traditional distinctions have recently come into question.[32]

No matter the stance one takes on the Homer question, that is, no matter whether one follows one standard answer or another, the contrast Nietzsche characterizes by distinguishing "the individual genius" from "the poetic spirit of a people" [*der dichterischen Volkseele*],[33] that is, between literary transmission on the basis of individual invention and, by contrast, a collective tradition of oral composition (Nietzsche remarks that with this question one apparently discovers "for the first time the wondrous capacity of the people's soul"),[34] makes it plain that the question has not changed in substance in the interim and despite its settled status. Nietzsche's critical insight is that the same "scientific" but no less "artistic," that is to say, specifically *aesthetic confidence*[35] justifies the argument within the discipline of classical philology on either side: "All these schools of thought start from the assumption that the problem of the present form of these epics can be solved from the standpoint of an aesthetic judgment."[36]

Nietzsche's reference to the person or "personality" (of Homer and of the scholar to boot) brings him in his subsequent writings to reflect upon education as such, not altogether unlike Illich, as Nietzsche conceived of the issue historically and structurally in his unpublished *On the Future of our Educational Institutions*. In his likewise unpublished "*Wir Philologen*," Nietzsche observes that the problem with philology is nothing but the very problem of education and hence the problem of the educators themselves (later he will turn his focus to the issue of culture and the capacity of an individual to acquire an education). Writing as ironically as one pleases, he notes: "Against the science of philology there would be nothing to say: yet the philologists are also the educators."[37] These reflections are subsequently published in his *Untimely Observations,* beginning with his pedagogic challenge to David Strauss and continuing with his reflection on the living use (and liability) of history and his *Schopenhauer as Educator.* These four reflections on theoretical religion or theology, comparative or hermeneutico-sociological history, theorizing and thematizing the exemplar and communal well being as well as his thoughts on musical culture, are inherently *educational* observations that should always be read together and against one another.

In *Schopenhauer as Educator* Nietzsche highlights the relevance of identifying an exemplar for one's formation as a question, as he also raises the issue of self-formation that will always be crucial to the one who makes Pindar's very pedagogic reflection, having *learned,* become the one you are.[38]

The idea of the ideal or the exemplar matters for Nietzsche not inevitably but in an all-too-human modality. One seeks an educator if only to spare oneself the trouble of educating oneself: "When the great thinker despises human beings, he despises their laziness: for it is on account of their laziness that men seem like manufactured goods, unimportant, and unworthy to be associated with or instructed" (SE §1). Nietzsche includes himself in this all-too-human accounting and discounting: "I believed that, when the time came, I would discover a philosopher to educate me, a true philosopher whom one could follow without any misgiving because one would have more faith in him than one had in oneself" (SE §2).

The project of educating oneself is not easy; also difficult is the task of finding for oneself an educator of the right kind: both undertakings presuppose the almost impossible imperative achievement of self-knowledge. Asking how we might begin to re-cognize ourselves, Nietzsche asks the more fundamental question of conscience as of one's unconscious dispositionality as a given enigma already compelling the practical necessity of the Delphic motto: "How can man know himself? He is a dark and veiled thing; and if the hare has seven skins, man can shed seventy times seven and still not be able to say: 'this is really you, this is no longer sloughed-off skin-layer' " (SE §1).

If Ivan Illich offers a "phenomenology" of school as a prelude to his deconstruction, as it were, of the same, Nietzsche undertakes a similarly and practically referred phenomenological hermeneutics of the self. To work out this epochal undertaking, as the path towards finding oneself, (again and to begin with): "Let the youthful soul look back on life with the question: what have you truly loved up to now, what has elevated your soul, what has mastered it and at the same time delighted it? Place these venerated objects before you in a row, and perhaps they will yield for you, through their nature and their sequence, a law, the fundamental law of your true self. Compare these objects, see how one complements, expands, surpasses, transfigures another, how they form a stepladder upon which you have climbed up to yourself as you are now; for your true nature lies, not hidden deep within you, but immeasurably high above you, or at least above that which you normally take to be yourself" (Ibid.).

As with any epoché, one seeks an elusive invariant. Here Nietzsche does not dispute the wisdom of the Delphic oracle, nor does he bracket Pindar's poetic challenge. Instead Nietzsche offers the task of cultivation not for its own sake but for the sake of a further liberation that he calls life: "Your true educators and formative teachers reveal to you what the real raw material of your being is, something quite ineducable, yet in any case accessible only with difficulty, bound, paralyzed: your educators can be only your liberators" (Ibid.). Here we see Nietzsche's great sympathy for both Spinoza and Pascal: "it is the perfecting of nature when it prevents her cruel and merciless attacks and turns them to good, when it draws a veil over the expressions of nature's stepmotherly disposition and her sad lack of understanding" (Ibid.). In this spirit Nietzsche comes to—or rather, and in a perfectly overdetermined modality for the Lutheran Augustinian, "finds"—himself reading Schopenhauer. Telling himself his own story in this way, Nietzsche undertakes the same kind of educational "cruising,"[39] to use Tracy Strong's calculatedly risqué language, just because it reflects the spirit of what we also read in the accounts of Descartes and Rousseau.

The seductiveness of this overtly confessional expression can obscure the earnest or vital necessity of the task Nietzsche saw before him both at the start of his call to Basel and in his sense of his own reflections as precisely, consummately *untimely*. Thus Nietzsche challenges our educational institutions: "What will not suffice, even among our noblest and best-instructed families, under the name of family tutor; what a collection of antiques and eccentrics is designating a grammar school and not found wanting; what are we not content with for a university —what leaders, what institutions, in comparison with the difficulty of the task of educating a man to be a man! Even the much admired way in which our German men of learning set about their scientific pursuits reveals above all that they are thinking more of science than they are of mankind, that they have been trained to sacrifice themselves to it like a legion of the lost, so as in turn to draw new generations on to the same sacrifice" (Ibid.).

Given this, and Nietzsche goes on to indict the political health of Germany, what Nietzsche finds in Schopenhauer is not the educator in rhetoric and style that one might have supposed (and rightly supposed given Schopenhauer's accomplishments as a stylist) nor indeed the educator in morals or virtue that seems to be traditional. By contrast, what Nietzsche finds is a spiritual and affective or intimate or friendly connection. Thus addressed, Nietzsche finds himself and just because he "took" Schopenhauer, however likely "foolish and immodest a way of putting it, *as though* it were for me he had written" (Ibid., emphasis added). Nietzsche goes on to observe, interrupting a complicatedly recurved sentence, that such a perceived personal affinity was possible just because what Schopenhauer did not do was to write for the sensibilities of his own times, that is to say, for the academic or scholarly concerns that might have ensured his own reception.

Here we are back to the element of seduction essential for every kind of pedagogic undertaking. What is needed is love and what love always needs is forbearance. Thus Nietzsche can characterize Schopenhauer's own and specifically non-stylized stylization by saying that "Shopenhauer never wants to cut a [rhetorical] figure: for he writes for himself. . . ." (Ibid.) The intimate vocative address speaks to the reader *as if, as though* there were no one else intended apart from the reader. Thus *writes* Nietzsche, our own educator (though we tend to skip Nietzsche's educators, not just Schopenhauer, in our impatience to take him as such). Here I cite the very beginning of David Allison's *Reading the New Nietzsche*: "Nietzsche writes for you, the reader, only you."[40] Nietzsche has company in this achievement. For the New Testament itself exemplifies a style of writing that is, *seemingly*, really, directed to you, you the reader, *only* you. Detailing this analysis in the second volume of *Human, All-too-Human*, writing of "the book that speaks of Christ" (HH II §98), Nietzsche consistently rebukes the Judeao-Christian tradition of the West with the charge that *Allerweltsbücher* reek of vulgarity. There is no other book that "expresses so candidly or contains such an abundance of that which does everybody good once in a while" (Ibid.). Both the candidness and "the joyful enthusiasm, ready for any sacrifice which we feel when we believe in and behold *our* 'truths' " (ibid.) are necessary. Addressed to everyone, a book for everyone is accordingly universal, and yet to have value it must at the same time be specifically, uniquely addressed to the reader. How can such a contradictory style of writing be achieved; how would this, how could this work?

The literal answer Nietzsche says (and the New Testament says this itself) is love. A word holds the secret to the writing of a book about the word of God: "subtlest artifice which Christianity has over the other religions is a word: it speaks of *love*" (HH II §95). The word "love" turns on, works by way of its uncannily metonymic allure: "There is in the word love something so ambiguous and suggestive, something which speaks to the memory and to future hope, that even the meanest intelligence and the coldest heart still feels something of the luster of this word" (Ibid.). This associative power, Nietzsche goes on to observe, affects both body and soul, however the listener may be sensually or else spiritually attuned. This metonymic conviction "proceeds from the idea that God could demand of man, his creature and likeness, only that which it is possible for the latter to accomplish" (HH II §96). Armed with this "confidence" (and whole metaphysical dominions, levels, and degrees of the same are involved in this), the believer is *able* to believe that "the commandment 'be ye perfect as your Father in Heaven is perfect' " can "in fact become a *life of bliss*. Error is thus able to make Christ's *promise* come true" (Ibid.).

The New Testament enables this erroneous conviction by way of its language and style. With sufficient perspicacity, Nietzsche reflects, one "can learn from it all the expedients by which a book can be made into a universal book, a friend of everyone, and especially that master expedient of representing everything as having already been discovered, with nothing still on the way and as yet uncertain" (HH II §98). I, the reader, am the intended addressee of this good news, as are you, and you, and you.

Where religious and self-help tracts follow the gospel, writing for and to everyone, Schopenhauer writes for himself, so Nietzsche says, and we get the sense that his subtitle to his Zarathustra, *A Book for All and None* is meant to go Schopenhauer one better. "*This is my way, where is yours?*" Here Nietzsche is pointing to more than the limited appreciation of his readers (although this theme too follows him throughout his life, finally to end in his *Ecce Homo* with the Galilean metaphor describing his writings as so many "fish hooks," and insisting on the absence of fish [EH, BGE §1] just as earlier he had spoken of "*The Missing Ear*" [HH, II §386], now with reference to Epictetus).

Writing *Schopenhauer as Educator*, Nietzsche invokes an author who would seem to have written *for* Nietzsche as reader, as learner. But such an affinity is possible because Schopenhauer's directed interlocutor is not the reader but and much rather Schopenhauer himself, qua excluded from the academy, that is, from the received scholarly mainstream of his day. Nietzsche's reflective point is that Schopenhauer benefits through his isolation (and we may recall by contrast that Strauss suffers in the context of the *Untimely Meditations* from his popularity, and so too, as Nietzsche will later argue, does Wagner). With this emphasis, Nietzsche's pedagogic focus is inevitably dedicated to those outside the mainstream like himself: the few, the rare. Nor is Schopenhauer's isolation an accidental detail. There can be no companionship save with one's own kind, where even a single friend, Nietzsche says, would be enough to bridge an abyss. Nietzsche's reference is to the Greek ideal of friendship, but he also points to the rare character of the philosopher as such. Most philosophers, Nietzsche will argue, have been solitaries. The idea of the married philosopher is laughable less because Nietzsche mocks the idea of marriage than because of its sheer implausibility. Marriage would have to be a consummate friendship, but friendship to begin with is *rare*.[41]

In addition to the inevitable dangers of Schopenhauer's isolation, there is also what Nietzsche calls "despair of the truth," a despair which, so he argues, haunts anyone who thinks through the problem of knowledge, the problem he names the "problem of science" (BT ii), qua problem or qua questionable, in his "Attempt at a Self-Critique" in his re-issue of the first book, renamed in Schopenhauer's honor, *The Birth of Tragedy: Or Hellenism and Pessimism*.

When Nietzsche recalls Kant's critical philosophy (and he could also have been speaking of his own didactic style) in his *Schopenhauer as Educator* with specific reference to the sensibility of the poet Heinrich von Kleist, he does so in order to explain Schopenhauer's reading of Kant in addition to the rare quality required in order to hear and to understand Kant, in spite of the common tendency to imagine that one has understood Kant already at work at the time of Nietzsche's writing or in the description of the age as neo-Kantian or the conviction that after Kant philosophy follows a new course. Nietzsche opposes this, emphasizing that, apart from Schopenhauer, few have understood what follows from Kant's writing precisely for philosophy, but *above all*, and this is his most dissonant and important point, for the sciences as a whole, especially the natural and formal sciences, particularly logic, particularly mathematics: "if the sciences are correct, then we no longer stand on Kant's foundation; if Kant is correct, then the sciences are incorrect" (KSA 7, 19 [125]).

Thus Nietzsche emphasizes: "it seems to me as though Kant really penetrated and radically transformed very few people at all. To be sure the work of this quiet scholar, as we can read everywhere, is said to have unleashed a revolution in all fields of intellectual inquiry, but I just can't believe that" (SE § 3). The foundational point quoted above from Nietzsche's unpublished notes regarding the natural sciences (where these sciences are traditionally supposed to have themselves been the inspiration for Kant's revolutionary program in philosophy) is that Kant's solution works at the expense of the natural sciences themselves. In the same way, and with regard to Kant's practical philosophy, Nietzsche argues that Kant wanted to prove the common man right in a manner incomprehensible to the same.[42]

What is required for the one for whom Schopenhauer could be an educator in the first place? What is the requisite intellectual and affective precondition for an understanding of Kant, which includes understanding (as did Schopenhauer, and as did Jacobi, etc.), the consequences of the Kantian critique? To be affected by Kant (or indeed by Schopenhauer or by Nietzsche)[43] in this way and in general—this would be the Kantian *überhaupt*—one needs in advance to be capable of grasping, precisely as not everyone is capable of grasping, the very revolutionary consequence of Kant's arguments with regard to nothing less than what Nietzsche named "the problem" per se "of science itself," that is, of science considered "for the first time as problematic, as questionable" (BT §ii).[44]

Such rare readers are exposed to doubt, to radical and vital doubt. Above such philosophical knights of the spirit, Nietzsche sets the *poets* who draw these same insights to their ultimate consequences. Such ultimately "active and noble spirits, those who could never endure living in a state of doubt, would experience a shattering and despair of all truth on the manner of Heinrich von Kleist" (ibid.). Nietzsche goes on to cite Kleist's description of the moral effects of the Kantian revolution in epistemology: " 'We cannot decide,' Kleist writes in a letter to a friend, 'whether what we call truth really is truth, or whether it only appears to us to be such. If the latter is the case, then the truth we collect here is nothing upon our death, and all our efforts to procure a possession that will follow us to the grave are in vain . . .' " (Ibid., cf. BT §15).[45] In parallel fashion, it is this same passion in moral philosophy that moves Schopenhauer when he proposes as the one rule of compassion *Neminem laede*, Injure no one, which for Schopenhauer requires more than the pity Nietzsche excoriates. Schopenhauer's moral ideal of loving kindness, and that is, of course, the plain meaning of compassion: *cause* or *make* no one suffer, *Neminem laede*, includes the corollary "*imo omnes, quantum potes, juva*"—*much rather help everyone as much as you can.* Compassion thus entails "the immediate participation independently of all ulterior considerations, primarily in the *suffering* of another, and thus in the prevention or elimination of it; for all satisfaction and all well-being and happiness consist in this."[46]

As Nietzsche explains in *On the Use and Disadvantage of History for Life*, "Few people truly serve the truth, because only a few people possess the pure will to be just, and of these even fewer possess the strength to be just" (HL §6). For Nietzsche, what matters is not the *will* as much as the capacity or power to *act.* Nietzsche's educational programme is accordingly practical rather than sentimental. When Nietzsche undertakes his *Schopenhauer as Educator*, he points to a series of difficulties in coming to know whether we have this rareness of character as well as the illusions and the obstacles that stand in the way of finding ourselves even when, perhaps especially when, we have such a rare nature. For it is not easy to reflect on ourselves, and reflection (or meditation or observation) out of time, untimely reflection, is not a neutral affair: "How easy it is" thereby, Nietzsche says, "to do damage to yourself that no doctor can heal. And moreover, why should it be necessary, since everything—our friendships *and* enmities, our look *and* our handshake, our memory *and* what we forget, our books *and* our handwriting—bears witness to our being" (SE §2; emphasis added).

Shadows at Midnight: Who is Nietzsche's *Übermensch*?

If Schopenhauer is Nietzsche's exemplar on the way to finding himself (and losing Schopenhauer in the process, as Zarathustra enjoins his followers to lose Zarathustra), Nietzsche's seeming ideal is the *Übermensch*. Not a few scholars have suggested this. In this next section, I examine this supposition and its limitations.

As an author, Nietzsche has an extraordinary relation to the shadow, deploying a range of variations of the German proverb: *no one jumps over his own shadow* (variations including inversion as his Zarathustra reflects, importantly to be found in the section following *On Self-Overcoming* and before section entitled *On the Land of Education*, "And only when he turns away from himself will he jump over his shadow—and verily into his own sun" (Z II *On Those who are Sublime*). And in a book that forms part of his *Human, All-too-Human*, "The Wanderer and his Shadow," a book conceived in and about chiaroscuro: the perceived play of shadows, of darkness and light, we should not forget that Zarathustra would be, as he often was, talking to himself, as hermits do, as wanderers do. Nietzsche, the thinker of the dawn and the late morning and noontide, of the coming of the twilight, or and most viscerally, sensually, of brown night and midnight, is not only referring to the shadow the thinker casts. For the wanderer is also a pilgrim on this earth and the shadow is the wanderer's soul: it goes on ahead of one, it follows, or it vanishes altogether.

On my own reading of the *Übermensch*, as what can appear to be Nietzsche's ideal, as the educational exemplar to beat all exemplars, I argue that we do well to keep Nietzsche's own education in mind. For in its Greek origins, speaking of Homer as of the Orphic or mystery tradition, the shadow, the shade is all that lives on in a subterranean translation, true even for a perished God, as Nietzsche observes in his *The Gay Science*. The didactic import of this reference works if one considers the Greek source of Nietzsche's *Übermensch*. For it is commonly assumed that Nietzsche's *Übermensch* corresponds, more or less coincidentally, more or less historically, to Hitler's fantasy: the evolutionary apex of human development. The *Übermensch* would be, if anyone would be, a *superior* human being (and that is also to say, with Plato and Aristotle and even Alasdair MacIntyre, a superior warrior or perfect soldier): the fruit of *science* or else *good breeding*, by which one means a family of a certain economic wherewithal, thereby heir to a certain "good" education, or "schooling" in Illich's sense, which as he reminds us presupposes nutrition, environment, travel, etc. This view is common stock among the Straussians.[47] Indeed, Straussian or not, the whole of technologically oriented society via the fantasy of genetic engineering and associated technologies as well as the fantasy life that is the internet and the media in general presupposes the same vision of the human per se and in general as supreme, as other, as "higher," in Nietzsche's words. Does Nietzsche preach this? Are we to make the way—and the earth—"free" for the overman to come?

I have argued that a hermeneutic reading suggests, per contra, that Nietzsche's Zarathustran overman may be anything but a goal or an advance.[48] In other words, when Nietzsche says in Zarathustra's mouth "I teach you the overman. Man is something that should be overcome" (Z, *Zarathustra's Prologue*, 2), he is talking about overcoming today's humanity. Hence as Zarathustra continues: "You have made your way from worm to man, and much in you is still worm. Once you were apes, and, even now, man is more of an ape" (Z, *Zarathustra's Prologue*, 3). The named relationship, it should be patent, between ape and man and hence the *contrasting* judgment once again echoes the Castor addendum to Pindar's second Pythian ode.[49] In this sense, after speaking (shades of Empedocles, and, here at least, shades of Emerson) of the need for purification—"What does your body say about your soul? Is your soul not poverty and dirt and a miserable ease? In truth, man is a polluted river." (Ibid.)—Zarathustra reflects on greatness as opposed to the image of such. In the next section on the "most contemptible man: the Ultimate man," we read first of surface "translations" as well as subterranean "translations" (just as Rohde treats of such translations in detail in succeeding chapters of his *Psyche* published in the years after Nietzsche's collapse):[50] "What is great in man is that he is a bridge and not a goal; what can be loved in man is that he is a going-across and a downgoing" (Z, *Zarathustra's Prologue*, 4).

Like the people to whom Zarathustra speaks, his words are not for our ears, not as we hear them today. Thus it is that both Nietzscheans and anti-Nietzscheans *believe* in the overman. *In potentia*, so we assume, we all *are* the overman, in some sense superior or higher human beings: by comparison with the slavely moral as we are also the dominant species in comparison with the ape (and every other living being).[51]

Thus the human, i.e. the all-too-human, *is* the overman. Nietzsche's point from start to finish is that we should get past these our unteachable stupidities, that we should overcome our human centered humanism.[52] In the concluding section below, I examine our still ongoing "lack" of philology (as Nietzsche would say) as this seems to account for what have been and still are the all-too-common (mis-)readings of the "superhuman" or *Übermensch*.

Between Nietzsche's *Übermensch* and Lucian's *Hyperanthropos*

This work is Lucian's, who well knew
The foolishness of times gone by,
For things the human race finds wise
Are folly to th' unclouded eye.

—Erasmus[53]

Every student of Nietzsche's work knows that the *Übermensch* is derived from Lucian of Samosata, a second-century Syrian and influential Greek stylist, author of numerous satirical dialogues plays, such as the *Dialogue of the Gods, The Dialogue of the Dead*, and the *Journey into Hell*. Scholars *know* this not because qua philologists like Nietzsche they know their Lucian but because Walter Kaufmann tells them so. Hence every account I have come across in English (as in German) dutifully reproduces Kaufmann's footnote (even when Kaufmann himself is not cited as the source).[54] There are Nietzsche scholars who refer to Lucian in connection with Nietzsche to be sure,[55] but on the *Übermensch*, as exemplar and ideal, apart from repeating Kaufmann's reference, no one has apparently bothered to return to the text itself. This inattention is regrettable as Lucian's *A Voyage to the Underworld or the Tyrant*[56] offers an intriguing insight into the notion of the *Übermensch*, specifically as considered in the context of Nietzsche's own "teaching" of the Overman in his *Thus Spoke Zarathustra*. Nietzsche's *Übermensch* is indebted to Lucian's *Hyperanthropos* in the Menippean fashion invoked at the conclusion of *Ecce Homo*, "What I owe the Ancients."[57]

The story Lucian tells in his play on the tyrant's *Untergang or going to ground* (in the extreme sense of the same), articulates the cautionary tale of those who are regarded in everyday as being "Higher-Men" but who are revealed as no more than or all-too-human when they cross over into the underworld (dragged as they are, kicking and screeching, into the afterlife just as the dwarf leaps over the tightrope walker or "overman" at the start of Zarathustra, and similarly threatens to drag him down into hell). The tyrant in Lucian's play is named Megapenthes, a king among men, superior politically and socially speaking, a man of power. Given such political excellence, the craftsman, a cobbler by trade, Mycillus confesses that he took the tyrant to be 'υπεράνθρωπός, "a superman, thrice blessed, better looking and a full royal cubit taller than almost anyone else."[58] But "when he was dead, not only did he cut an utterly ridiculous figure in my eyes on being stripped of his pomp, but I laughed at myself even more than at him because I had marveled at such a worthless creature, inferring his happiness from the savour of his kitchen and counting him lucky because of his purple derived from the blood of mussels in the Laconian sea."[59] Lucian then goes on to mock the moneylenders, and so on (and on).

Beyond Rohde's *Psyche* (although Rohde himself does not emphasize the concept of the overman in Lucian),[60] and beyond Lucian's antique rhetoric, how are we to understand Nietzsche's overman, as this notion has been one of the most dangerously influential of all? In its Aryan configuration, set into what some claim to have been its original constellation in Nietzsche's *Der Wille zur Macht* (that infamously "invented" book), the idea of the *Übermensch* has been regarded as the causal factor not only in Hitler's war but also the first world war (which was itself also called, instructively, fatally enough, "Nietzsche's war" by journalists of the day).[61] In other words, talking about Nietzsche's *Übermensch*, we seem to be talking about the philosophy that generated the language of the master-race, that is, the *Übermensch* as opposed to the *Unter-Mensch* as Nazi terminology also speaks of it. Nietzsche, to be sure, uses both terms. Yet as I argue here and as so I hope, the reference to Lucian should make plain (as Nietzsche's own emphasis on the rhetorical importance of Mennipean satire might also make this patent as well as his repeated plays on Zarathustra: *now* as tragedy, *now* as comedy, *now* as parody), Nietzsche's Zarathustra teaches the *Übermensch* in an ironic fashion that depends upon its parodic allusion to Lucian and thus to the prospect of death, as in this life we are over or above the earth or dust where we shall, each of us, end. To say that the teaching of the *Übermensch* is ironic does *not mean* that Nietzsche's Zarathustra does not teach the *Übermensch*—of course he does.

Thus one can fail to note (certainly even many sophisticated and sensitive Nietzsche scholars do so) that the elusive doctrine of the eternal return, the doctrine that Zarathustra comes to teach, namely the teaching that the overman himself or herself is meant to be the passage toward, is the eternal return of the *same* and this truth of recurrence is a truth of life *and* death. Related to Empedocles' "truth" of rebirth, Nietzsche's Zarathustra teaches that the human is charged to overcome or to get over the human. No one can jump over his own shadow, says the proverb, yet, as we recall again: the one who is sublime learns to jump over his own shadow and thereby springs into his own sunlight.

These days we have a number of readings of the posthuman, overhuman, transhuman. Recent scholarship inspired more by (Anglophone readings of) French (rather than German) philosophical and sociological thought (i.e., readings of Bergson, Lefebvre, Simondon, Deleuze, Foucault) take this argument to what such scholars like to call the "trans-human" condition—more Donna Haraway than Hannah Arendt—and it is thus a pro-cybernetic move in the direction if not of the robotic, then at the least of the very modest "cyborg" that is a kid texting a friend, a man masturbating with an internet connection, or just contact lenses, or a pacemaker, or what have you. But Nietzsche is not talking about cyborgs or transhumans as much as he is—this is where the reference to the becoming of life is essential—talking about humans *and* other animals. For Nietzsche is not persuaded that we are, as he says, either "other" or "higher" than the animals. In this sense, one might want to consider the kinship with nature that can make us accuse Nietzsche of a Goethean *Naturmystik* but, and even then, we would miss the point Nietzsche seeks to underscore with his *Übermensch*, if we can permit ourselves to take it as a satirical expression.[62]

By now it should be a bit more evident that context makes all the difference, not just for Nietzsche but for Lucian. For Lucian's provocative contrast highlights the superficial vision of the overman, the man of the upper or wealthy classes, as a man who towers above others regarded as lower, or lesser, in this life, and the very *same* man translated or transposed into the afterlife, a contrast illuminated, as it were, in the darkness rather than the light of eternity.

This opposition belongs to what I have named Nietzsche's *reflection* on perspective per se and not his "perspectivism" as analysts of all stripes insist on saying, but his *perspectivalism*, given the values we have in our culture and context as contrasted with our tendency to take these values not only as universal but as timeless or essential. For as Nietzsche reminded his readers in his reflection on his own catalogue of his published books that is his *Ecce Homo*, "Ultimately, nobody can get more out of things, including books, than he already knows. For what one lacks access to from experience one will have no ear" (EH, *Why I write such good books*, §1). As an exemplification of the mirage that stands in the place of understanding, the reader who merely makes "something" of Nietzsche "out of his own image," by contrast with those who understand nothing at all and thereby contending that he need not be "considered at all," Nietzsche invokes the misunderstanding of the *Ubermensch* as a prime example of such misprision. Conceived, so Nietzsche writes here, "as the designation of a type of supreme achievement," the "word 'overman'" has been misunderstood "as an 'idealistic' type of a higher kind of man, half 'saint,' half 'genius'" (Ibid.). It is no accident that Nietzsche here goes on to denounce those "other scholarly oxen" who accuse him "of Darwinism" on that very same account.

There is more than a small bit of education that would be needed for such a perspectivalist perspective on perspective. It is in this sense that we will conclude by remarking on the substance of Nietzsche's reflection on the value of the thinker as educator for life, precisely "as one who has educated himself and who thus knows how it is done" (SE §1). For Nietzsche, writing here and throughout his reflections on education as a thinker: "one should speak only of self-education. The education of youth by others is either an experiment carried out on an as yet unknown and unknowable subject, or a leveling on principle with the object of making the new being, whatever it may be, conform to the customs and habits then prevailing: in both cases therefore something unworthy of the thinker, the world of those elders and teachers whom a man of rash honesty once described as *nos ennemis naturels*" (HH, *The Wanderer and his Shadow*, §267).

We are hardly beyond the imperative need as Illich had identified it to de-school society, the need to go beyond sheer indoctrination, even for the sake of the possible experiment of drawing youth beyond itself and what it supposes itself to know about. In the process, it is my hope that we include Nietzsche's critical reflection on the role of the thinker and the need to read references (when one bothers to have any at all), just because "*There are no educators.—*" (Ibid.) We still have to overspring the shadow of tradition; we have not yet managed to leap into our own light.

Notes

[1] Ivan Illich, *Deschooling Society* (London: Marion Boyars Publishers Ltd., 2000).

[2] I lack the space here to detail this parallel, but an illustration can be found in Illich, *In the Vineyard of the Text* (Chicago: University of Chicago Press, 1993).

[3] Ellul names education the very foundation of propaganda, in the sense of being the precondition for it in the first place. Ellul, *Propaganda: The Formation of Men's Attitudes* (New York: Vintage Books, 1973), 108.

[4] "[I]t is only normal that the most educated people (intellectuals) are the first to be reached by such propaganda. . . . All this runs counter to pat notions that only the public

swallows propaganda. Naturally, the educated man does not *believe* in propaganda; he shrugs and is convinced that propaganda has no effect on him. This is, in fact, one of his great weaknesses, and propagandists are well aware that in order to reach someone, one must first convince him that propaganda is ineffectual and not very clever. Because he is convinced of his own superiority, the intellectual is much more vulnerable than anybody else to this maneuver." Ellul, *Propaganda*, 111.

[5] Illich, *Deschooling Society*, 42. Iraq and Afghanistan substitute today for Illich's Vietman, and we note, with sorrow, that we have ceased even to count enemy deaths.

[6] See Ellul's *The Technological Society*, trans. John Wilkinson (New York: Knopf, 1964) [*La Technique, Ou, L'enjeu Du Siecle*, (Paris: Armand Colin, 1954)] and *The Technological System*, trans. Joachim Neugroschel (New York: Continuum, 1980) [*Le système technician* (Paris: Calmann-Lévy, 1977)].

[7] Illich, *Deschooling Society*, 52. "I believe that a desirable future depends on our deliberately choosing a life of action over a life of consumption, on our engendering a life style which will enable us to be spontaneous, independent, yet related to each other, rather than maintaining a life style which only allows us to make and unmake, produce and consume—a style of life which is merely a way station on the road to the depletion and pollution of the environment. The future depends more upon our choice of institutions which support a life of action than on our developing new ideologies and technologies." Ibid., 52–3.

[8] Ibid., 67.

[9] *Human, All-too-Human*, I: §481. References to Nietzsche's texts are abbreviated and cited by section number or title (rather than the page of any given edition).

[10] See, for example, Paulo Freire, *Pedagogy of the Oppressed* (New York: Continuum, 2000). See for a discussion of Freire and Illich (and it is to be noted that, even on the left, a focus on Freire for educational theorists often excludes Illich), Richard Kahn, "Critical Pedagogy Taking the Illich Turn," *The International Journal of Illich Studies*, Vol. 1, No. 1, (2009) 37–49.

[11] Illich, "An Address to 'Master Jacques,'" *Bulletin of Science Technology & Society* 14 (2) (1994), 65–8. See Ellul, *The Technological Society* (New York: Knopf, 1964) originally published as *La Technique, Ou, L'enjeu Du Siecle*, (Paris: Armand Colin, 1954).

[12] Gadamer's discussion of his understanding of language and conversation by contrast with Heidegger's understanding is valuable here. See Gadamer, "Heidegger as Rhetor: Hans-Georg Gadamer as Interviewed by Ansgar Kemmann," in Daniel M. Gross and Kemmann, eds., *Heidegger and Rhetoric* (Albany: State University of New York Press, 2005), 47–64, here: 50ff, esp. 51.

[13] Jaeger explicated the term as "the shaping of the Greek character." See *Paideia: The Ideals of Greek Culture, Volume I: Archaic Greece. The Mind of Athens*, trans. Gilbert Highet (Oxford: Oxford University Press, 1965), ix.

[14] As Illich notes: "With very rare exceptions, the university graduate from a poor country feels more comfortable with his North American and European colleagues than with his nonschooled compatriots, and all students are academically processed to be happy only in the company of fellow consumers of the products of the educational machine." *Deschooling Society*, 34. Illich's point should be integrated with the tendency of any interlocutor to except himself from the equation even as he acknowledges injustice and exclusion. Cf. Peggy McIntosh, "White Privilege: Unpacking the Invisible Knapsack," in Paula S. Rothenberg, ed., *Race, Class, and Gender in the United States: An Integrated Study* (Worth Publishers, 2003 [1988]), 192–9.

[15] See Bourdieu, *Distinction: A Social Critique of the Judgment of Taste* (Cambridge: Harvard University Press, 1987). It is common for academics to pretend that there are no such distinctions, especially academics not employed at schools that are supposed "distinguished." But even such academics are able (all of them are) to "rate" schools and departments and their own students and colleagues. Some even undertake to post these ratings on the internet. One can read Nietzsche against such ambitions but it will do to read Bruce Wilshire's *Fashionable Nihilism: A Critique of Analytic Philosophy* (Albany: SUNY Press, 2002) or David Hoekhema's review of the same in the *Notre Dame Philosophical Review* (10.4.2002) in addition to the disparate range of contributions, including my own, to Carlos Prado's edited collection, *A House Divided: Comparing Analytic and Continental Philosophy* (Amherst, NY: Prometheus/Humanity Books, 2003).

[16] Illich was vice-rector of the Catholic University of Ponce in Puerto Rico from 1956–1960.

[17] Illich, *H2O and the Waters of Forgetfulness* (Dallas: Institute of Humanities and Culture, 1985).

[18] See on computers in primary schooling, Clifford Stoll, *High Tech Heretic: Why Computers Don't Belong in the Classroom and Other Reflections by a Computer Contrarian* (New York: Doubleday, 1999).

[19] As if one's *alma mater* were ever anything more than an accidental bystander in the individual's passing from adolescence to early adulthood.

[20] Illich, *Deschooling Society*, 18.

[21] Illich, *Deschooling Society*, 1.

[22] Thus it is a testimony to Ellul himself that he engages Jean Baudrillard, just for one example of Ellul's scholarship, long before today's scholarly interest in Baudrillard, just as Dominque Janicaud points to Simondon in advance of today's enthusiasm for philosophizing *with* rather than *against* (as one continues to imagine that these distinctions are intellectually decisive) technology. Ellul's engagement with Baudrillard distinguishes his own approach from Baudrillard, but he also recognizes the contribution Baudrillard makes and such a level of reception with regard to Ellul is often missing among the Baudrillard scholars who are now emerging in the wake of Baudrillard's death. For his own part, Domique Janicaud is thus the rare author who writes on technology and society in a sense informed by Ellul. There are of course other exceptions in the philosophy of technology. See for an exemplification and overview, John M. Staudenmaier, S. J., "Rationality, Agency, Contingency: Recent Trends in the History of Technology," *Reviews in American History* 30 (1) (2002), 168–81.

[23] See Lonergan's *Insight: A Study of Human Understanding* (New York: Philosophical Library, 1968). As Lonergan expressed this point rather pithily in class, "nobody teaches, if nobody learns."

[24] As Illich writes, rather than instruction or learning *per se*, "selection for a role or category in the job market increasingly depends on mere length of attendance." *Deschooling Society*, 11.

[25] Never mind that we all have such degrees and write such letters of our own (and should for just this reason know better), I will not be the only one to have observed an academic process where such an argument from authority has been deployed to settle doubts about publication record (or indeed in place of an evaluation of the quality of the same).

[26] Nietzsche, "Homer und die klassische Philologie" (1869), in *Sämtliche Werke*, Giorgio Colli and Mazzino Montinari, eds. (Berlin: de Gruyter, 1982), Vol. II/1 *Philologische Schriften 1867–1873*, 247–69. Cf. "Notizen/ zu/ Wir Philologen," in Nietzsche, *Kritische Studienausgabe* (Berlin: de Gruyter, 1980), Vol. 8, 14ff.

[27] "[F]or they alone can judge how the sword of barbarism sweeps over the head of every one who loses sight of the unutterable simplicity and noble dignity of the Hellene; and how no progress in commerce or technical industries, however brilliant, no school regulations, no political education of the masses, however widespread and complete, can protect us from the curse of ridiculous and barbaric offenses against good taste, or from annihilation by the dreadfully beautiful Gorgon head of the classicist." "Nietzsche, Homer und die klassische Philologie," 251.

[28] As Nietzsche explains: "the zenith of the historical-literary studies of the Greeks, and hence also of their point of greatest importance—i.e., the 'Homer question'—was reached in the age of the Alexandrian grammarians." Ibid., 255.

[29] Nietzsche, "Homer und die klassische Philologie," 253.

[30] This is a literal if periphrastic characterization: "im Namen der Philologie selbst, die zwar weder eine Muse noch eine Grazie, aber eine Götterbotin ist." "Nietzsche, Homer und die klassische Philologie," 269.

[31] See Babich, "Nietzsche's Philology and Nietzsche's Science: On The 'Problem of Science' and '*fröhliche Wissenschaft*,'" in Pascale Hummel, eds., *Metaphilology: Histories and Languages of Philology* (Paris: Philologicum, 2009), 155–201.

[32] I note here the problems of classification which are difficult enough when one could speak of prose and poetic styles in antiquity but confounded for philosophy in great measure by recent discoveries, particularly but not only the Derveni papyrus. For a conventional representation of interpretive accounts, see the contributions to A. Laks and G. Most, eds., *Studies on the Derveni Papyrus* (Oxford: Oxford University Press, 1997).

[33] The sentence in its entirety asks: "Giebt es charakteristische Unterschiede zwischen den Aeusserungen des *genialen Individuums* und der *dichterischen Volksseele*?" "Nietzsche, Homer und die klassische Philologie," 252, 296.

[34] Ibid., 248; cf. 254.

[35] This artistic emphasis is highlighted at the very start of Nietzsche's lecture as belonging to the science of philology.

[36] Ibid.

[37] "Gegen die Wissenschaft der Philologie wäre nichts zu sagen: aber die Philologen sind auch die Erzieher." Nietzsche, KSA 8, 3 [3], 14.

[38] Nietzsche (as we know) leaves out this *having learned*. Elsewhere I argue that he takes this "having learned" as the point of departure for his Zarathustran imperative: *Werde der du bist, [Having learned—, having been experienced—, having been tried—] become the one you are.* To the same extent that Pindar's *Become the one you are* is agonistic through and through, it can be understood as an imperative of praise or celebration: at once descriptive and prescriptive. See Babich, "Become the One You Are: On Commandments and Praise—Among Friends," in Thomas Hart, ed., *Nietzsche, Culture, and Education* (London: Ashgate, 2009), 13–38.

[39] Thus Nietzsche writes: "I still lacked this philosopher, and I tried this one and that one" (Ibid., §2) See Tracy B. Strong, footnote 20 to his new introduction to the second edition of *Friedrich Nietzsche and the Politics of Transfiguration* (Bloomington: University of Indiana Press, 2000), xxx.

[40] David B. Allison, *Reading the New Nietzsche* (Lanham: Rowman and Littlefield, 2001), 1.

[41] See the section entitled "Of Friends" in *Human, All too Human*, and compare with his discussion of the friend in *Thus Spoke Zarathustra*. The problem turns upon perception and representation—or truth and lie—among friends. Where he ends this section (entitled "Man in Society") with the short verse: "'Friends, there are no friends!' thus said the dying sage / Foes, there are no foes, say I, the living fool." (HH I §376), he goes on in the next section to emphasize that "Fellow rejoicing [*Mitfreude*], not fellow suffering [*Mitleid*], makes the friend" (HH I §499).

[42] See the aphorism entitled "Kant's Joke" (GS §193).

[43] Nietzsche is always talking about Nietzsche, which does not mean that he is not also talking about Schopenhauer and Kant.

[44] See Babich, *Nietzsche's Philosophy of Science: Reflecting Science on the Ground of Art and Life* (Albany: State University of New York Press, 1994) just to begin with.

[45] I develop this point further in Babich, "*Ex aliquo nihil*: Nietzsche on Science and Modern Nihilism," *American Catholic Philosophical Quarterly. Special Issue on Nietzsche.* Vol. 84, No. 2 (Spring 2010): 231–56.

[46] Schopenhauer, *On the Basis of Morality*, trans. E. F. J. Payne (Providence: Berghahn Books, 1995), 144.

[47] See, just for instance: Michael Allen Gillespie, "'Slouching Toward Bethlehem to Be Born': On the Nature and Meaning of Nietzsche's Superman," *The Journal of Nietzsche Studies* 30 (2005), 49–69, and Lawrence Lambert's *Nietzsche's Teaching: An Interpretation of "Thus Spoke Zarathustra"* (New Haven: Yale University Press, 1989).

[48] It is not that it has never occurred to anyone that the *Übermensch* might be a parodic concept: among others Keith Ansell-Pearson argues that Nietzsche lays out a parodic path his 1886 preface to *Human, All Too Human*. "Toward the *Übermensch:* Reflections on the Year of Nietzsche's Daybreak," *Nietzsche-Studien* 23 (1994), 128–30. Richard Perkins sees these figures as the lover, the knower, and the creator in his "How an Ape Becomes a Superman: Notes on a Parodic Metamorphosis in Nietzsche," *Nietzsche-Studien* 15 (1986), 180. Here I seek to attend to the classical echoes of parody and note that without underscoring the parodic dimension, Marie-Luise Haase sees the figures of the *Übermensch* as saint, philosopher, and artist: "Der Übermensch in Also Sprach Zarathustra und im Zarathustra Nachlass, 1882–1885," *Nietzsche-Studien* 13 (1984), 236. Eugen Fink argues for the genius, the free spirit, and Zarathustra himself, *Nietzsches Philosophie* (Stuttgart: Kohlhammer, 1960), 72ff.

[49] Babich, "Pindar's Becoming" in Babich, *Words in Blood, Like Flowers: Philosophy and Poetry, Music and Eros in Hölderlin, Nietzsche, and Heidegger* (Albany: State University of New York Press, 2006), 75–94.

[50] See Rohde, *Psyche: The Cult of Souls and the Belief in Immortality among the Greeks*, trans. W. B. Hillis (London: Routledge and Kegan Paul, 1925), originally published 1890–1894.

[51] Or else if not yet by ordinary or natural evolutionary means, then certainly on the model that some scientist must currently be developing using the latest genetic or stem cell technology, further transforming us in the same direction that we already find ourselves going.

[52] Note that when Heidegger accuses Nietzsche of just these errors in his *Letter on Humanism* addressed to Jean Beaufret and elsewhere, it is to save the insight as his own rather than as Nietzsche's. Nietzsche's rhetorical style, and Heidegger's didactic acuity, meant that he knew that at least some readers would tolerate this misreading to his benefit.

[53] After Christopher Robinson, *Lucian and his Influence in Europe*, citing the epigram to Aldine edition of Erasmus, *In Praise of Folly* (Chapel Hill: The University of North Carolina Press, 1979), 191.

[54] The footnote is easy to find and very simple, "*Kataplous*, 16." See Kaufmann, *Nietzsche, Philosopher, Psychologist, Antichrist* (Princeton: Princeton University Press, 1974), 307, note 1. Kaufman's main text explained that "The *hyperanthropous* is to be found in the writings of Lucian in the second-century AD and Nietzsche as a classical philologist had studied Lucian and made frequent references to him in his philologia." Ibid. Erkme Joseph, *Nietzsche im "Zauberberg"* (Frankfurt am Main: Klostermann, 1996) duly cites Kaufmann in his notes before going on to detail the earlier appearances of the term *Übermensch* as such in German, 271ff. But prior to Kaufmann, see the entry in Rudolf Eisler's *Handwörterbuch der Philosophie* (Berlin: Mittler und Sohn, 1913) as well as Ernst Benz: "Das Bild des Übermenschen in der Europäischen Geistesgeschichte" in his *Der Übermensch. Eine Diskussion* (Stuttgart: Rhein-Verlag 1961), 16–19. Similar details, drawn from Kaufmann, appear in Karen Joisten, cited below, and so too with reference to anthropology and the social sciences Jyung-Hyun Kim, *Nietzsches Sozialphilosophie: Versuch einer Überwindung der Moderne im Mittelpunkt des Begriffes Leib* (Würzburg: Königshausen and Neumann, 1995), Note 239, 198ff. See for a politicized overview, Ulrich Busch, "Vergessene Utopien: Friedrich Nietzsches Vision vom Übermenschen," *Utopie kreativ*, 151 (Mai 2003), 460–667.

[55] I note Anke Bennholdt-Thommsen as well as Gary Shapiro, Robin Small, and Kathleen Higgins who pays special attention (as others do) to Apuleius. But one tends not to refer to Lucian and those who do (again on the *hyperanthropos* question) do not invoke the context.

[56] See the Loeb edition: *Lucian in Eight Volumes*, trans. A. M. Harman (Cambridge: Harvard University Press, 1968 [1915]), Vol. II, 1–57, or the Everyman library edition, translated by Lionel Casson, *Selected Satires of Lucian* (New York: Norton, 1968), 175–93.

[57] In addition to Bakhtin, Northrop Frye had already laid the ground rules or gone to the grounds, or, still better, to the underground for English readers, explaining in a section of his *Anatomy of Criticism* entitled "Theory of Myths"—just because, rhetorically, and given the distance between our own time and Lucian and Menippus, but also Nietzsche himself, it really *needs* explaining—that "whenever the 'other world' appears in satire, it appears as an ironic counterpart to our own, a reversal of accepted social standards. This form of satire is represented in Lucian's *Kataplous* and *Charon*, journeys to the other world in which the eminent in this one are shown doing appropriate but unaccustomed things, a form incorporated in Rabelais, and in the medieval *danse macabre*. In the last named the simple equality of death is set against the complex inequalities of life." Frye, *Anatomy of Criticism: Four Essays* (Princeton: Princeton University press, 1957), 232.

[58] [. . . 'υπεράνθρωπος τις α ̓νὴρ καὶ τρισόβιός μοι κατεφαίνετο καὶ μονονουχὶ πάντων καλλίων καὶ 'υψηλ ότερος 'όλω πήχει βασιλικῶ . . .]. *Lucian in Eight Volumes*, Vol. II, "The Downward Journey," 34/35. Cf. Lucian's "Menippus or the Descent into Hades" where Croesus complains to Pluto that Menippus is giving them a hard time in hell. Menippus replies: "Pluto, it's true, I hate them. They're spineless good-for-nothings. . . . I enjoy needling them." But Pluto notes, "But you shouldn't. They left a great deal behind. That's why they take it to heart." Menippus is adamant, and Croesus cries "This is terrible!" to which Menippus retorts: "It is not. But what you people used to do on the earth was. Making people grovel before you, lording it over free men, never giving the slightest thought to death. Well you can start whimpering because you've lost it all." *Selected Satires of Lucian*,

212–13. Cf. Nietzsche, HH, *Mixed Opions and Maxims* 1879 § 408 and Erwin Rohde, *Der griechische Roman und seine Vorläufer* (Leipzig: Breitkopf und Härtel, 1900). For Lucian's influence, see further Herbert Hunger, *Die hochsprachliche profane Literatur der Byzantiner; Teilbd. 2: Philologie, Profandichtung, Musik, Mathematik und Astronomie, Naturwissenschaften, Medizin, Kriegswissenschaft, Rechtsliteratur* (München: Beck, 1978), 151f., as well as Christopher Robinson, *Lucian and his Influence in Europe* (London: Duckworth, 1979) and more broadly, Werner von Koppenfels, *Der andere Blick. Das Vermächtnis des Menippos in der europäischen Literatur* (München: C.H. Beck, 2007). A rewarding treatment is Francis G. Allinson, *Lucian: Satirist and Artist* (Boston: Marshall Jones Company, 1926) who for his own part refers both to Rohde's studies and to Swift's objectly "Lucianic" debt to Lucian.

59 Ibid.

60 Thus perhaps we are right to read Nietzsche's Zarathustra, and to esteem Nietzsche above Rohde, yet Alan Cardew argues, per contra, that we might invert the order. See Cardew, "The Dioscuri: Nietzsche and Erwin Rohde," in Paul Bishop, *Nietzsche and Antiquity* (Rochester: Boydell and Brewer, 2004), 458–78.

61 See William Macintire Salter, "Nietzsche and War," in Tracy Strong, ed., *Friedrich Nietzsche* (Aldershot: Ashgate, 2009), 3–26. See also Strong's overall "Introduction" (Ibid., xi–xxxiii) to the question of war and the political and my own discussion of Salter in Babich, "Nietzsche's Will to Power: Politics and Destiny," ibid., 281–96.

62 Cf. Nietzsche HH, *Mixed Opinions and Maxims* 1879 § 408 and, again, Rohde, *Der griechische Roman und seine Vorläufer.*

Index